AF288125

From man to man

The truth about men in midlife crisis

My guide with an unsparing look at a phase of life

Why am I writing this book?

Confucius says: Even the longest journey begins with the first step. I had to get over myself to start this book. Firstly, because I didn't really feel like dealing with everything, and secondly, because I was afraid of the huge amount of work involved in this book. It was only at my wife's insistence that I was able to tackle this book and I hope it helps you.

It was a difficult journey and a gradual process that imperceptibly turns you into something else, and that is not necessarily a good thing. If you feel the way I describe in this book, behave the same way or learn from my mistakes and do better.

Losing everything just because of a few damn hormones isn't worth it. So, guys, read on and take care of yourselves. If you've bought this book or received it as a gift, you're or were probably just like me:

midlife crisis or menopause. Even before we go to the urologist at the age of 50, we have already experienced a lot.

We freak out over every little thing, feel ill, think we have a fever because we feel like we're burning up, and then suddenly everything is fine again. We can no longer sleep, are constantly restless, have constant flashes of thoughts and can no longer find our balance. This rollercoaster ride is exhausting, gruelling and has also pushed me to my limits.

Life changes during these years. To give you an insight into a man's menopause and what I've been through, I'll tell you my story: my fear of death, manhood and the total loss of my marriage. I would never have thought that it would also affect us men.

There are many books about a woman's menopause, but no guides for us men. This topic is taboo for men and talking about it is frowned upon. It is not even discussed among good friends. The image of the constantly strong and controlled man falls apart when we openly admit that we are not invulnerable either. I want to put an end to this and show you what I have experienced and how you too can deal with this sensitive topic. You see, you're not alone. The menopause is a tough time full of changes. Repressing it under the motto "It doesn't happen to us men" is not a solution.

Today, I see the menopause in men with different eyes. Looking back, I ask myself what was wrong with me and why I didn't deal with the issue. It was pride, it was ignorance and perhaps also fear of the unknown. You have to take your time and not work against it, because in the end you can say that things can only get better. There is life after the menopause. Life goes on. For me, it was with a new love for my wife.

The menopause is a gradual process that I didn't notice. It started for me at 49, I became unbalanced, moody, quick-tempered and impulsive. Sexual aversion and loss of fitness were the result. I, who had always been sporty and looked after my body, suddenly saw my muscles give way and my energy dwindle. I would like to warn men who think they are too cool for these issues: this change catches up with everyone.

There were constant arguments and disputes with my customers. I was self-employed as a web designer and photographer for 30 years. Anyone who got on my nerves even a little bit felt my aggression. Disputes often culminated in pure hatred and ended up with a lawyer. I didn't want to be bullied, neither in my private life nor at work. A gentler way never occurred to me. The warrior in me drew a broadsword and, metaphorically speaking, hit others in the skull. My wife felt the full brunt of my aggression on those days and I took my anger out on her. In short, I was a complete arsehole.

I was no longer open to reasonable arguments, even though my wife often only wanted to help me and protect me with her loving nature. If I had heeded her advice, I would have been spared money for lawyers and courts, as well as angry customers and friends. But the bastard was the greatest and everyone else was just maggots. But I didn't reflect on all that.

Whinging is for sissies, I told myself. Negative thoughts were catching up with me more and more often. Even things from my school days and youth came to the surface, people who had annoyed me or treated me unfairly. I hated them all. Depression, lack of sleep and anger plagued me. The next moment I was in a great mood again. A constant up and down of emotions. Something had to change fundamentally. I wanted to get back what I had lost in my youth and experience all the things I had on my bucket list before the lid closed. So I made a decision.

The menopause is a gradual, imperceptible process that has changed the way I think and act. But it is also a turning point. A moment when you the chancehave to understand yourself better and redefine yourself. I'm getting everything off my chest to show you: There is an after. And it can be a damn good after if you take the first step.

You are the sum of your past experiences

In the first decade of the 2000s, I was a real workaholic. I had several companies running: a financial advisory agency, a property company and a web design business. Financially, things were excellent. I was a cocky, arrogant monkey. If you've ever seen the film "Wolf of Wall Street" - I was like Jordan Belfort, just the biggest (the biggest jerk).

But for 30,000 euros a month, I also had to work seven days a week. During the week, I kept the finance and web business running and at the weekend I carried out viewings for the property company. Our sons were born at the same time in 1998 and 2001, and to top it all off, my first wife wanted a house at that time. Simply so that the kids wouldn't have to grow up in the city and would have a nice environment.

No sooner said than done: we bought a house on the outskirts of Berlin, but it was only half-finished. There was still a lot of work to be done. Only the roof and the façade were actually finished. All our relatives advised us not to buy this house, especially my father-in-law. The house was basically a shell. He realised immediately that this house would become a million-dollar grave. I grew up in the country and had some manual labour experience. My father-in-law knew that, but he also realised how much work would have to be put into this house. But the location and style of the house, as well as the large plot, were a strong argument in favour of buying it. The house was very large, with almost 300 square metres of living space. The living room alone was 120 square metres, with a window front across the entire width and a view of the forest. The living room was very high due to the pitched roof, around seven metres, and had a gallery running around the top. That was a real eye-catcher.

The seller was a shady bloke who was on the verge of bankruptcy and was divorced. The fact that we didn't "get to the bottom" of this guy before buying the house was to take bitter revenge.

My wife at the time really wanted the house and urged me to speak to my bank. I wanted to have an appraisal done in advance, but she was against it and urged me to buy almost every day. The bank gave its approval for DM 375,000 within a few days. As I was earning well at the time, a monthly instalment of 1700 DMwas no problem.

We then moved into the house in mid-2000. I started renovating straight away and finished off room after room. I worked on the house after work or in the morning, then went to work and came home late at night.

These were usually ten to twelve-hour days. I'm very good with my hands as I grew up in the countryside and my father taught me a lot. So I could do almost everything except tiling, which was always too fiddly for me, I didn't fancy it. I even built the fireplace in the living room all by myself

There were actually DIY kits back then - a bit like Lego for adults, only without the fun and in XXL. You can imagine it like this: They deliver you a huge pallet of aerated concrete blocks, bags of plaster, a few marble benches and a monstrous cast-iron insert. Oh yes, and to top it all off, there was a VHS video. It explained every step as if you could do it in your sleep. Not at all!

You really had to do everything yourself: Cutting the stones to size, fitting the pieces together precisely, and then lifting those darn heavy marble benches that were so bulky you thought they came from an ancient temple.

But I wouldn't have been me if I had let that get me down. With a home-made pulley block - yes, the thing was really home-made - I pulled the whole thing up on my own. No help from friends, no neighbourly help, nothing. Just me, my will and this incredibly heavy monster.

I swear, when I was finally finished, I felt like a bloody hero. Anyone who sees the thing today probably thinks: "Oh, that must have been a professional." But no, it was me. A guy with a VHS tape and a good dose of madness!

The chimney sweep was thrilled at the inspection, he couldn't believe that I had managed to do this for the first time and on my own.

But now back to the subject of buying a house.

The first problems occurred just a few weeks after the purchase. It was raining in. We called in a roofer, who discovered that part of the shingle roof was damaged, which the seller had of course concealed from us. And this is where the hasty purchase without a survey took its revenge.

The end of the story: a new roof for 18,000.was needed But it didn't stop there. Every project I tackled in this house turned into an odyssey. No matter where you started to open or uncover something, it was always a mess. The previous owner obviously only knew building foam, cable ties, armour tape and silicone as building materials.DM

In the end, the house cost me a total of 795,000 euros by the time I moved out in 2008. I could have got a brand new period house for that. It was the biggest money-grab of my life. It really bothered me, my savings melted away and so did my pension provision. At the time, I didn't realise that I wouldn't receive more than 165,000 euros for the house and I couldn't even imagine it.

I couldn't work as much as I had to earn money to keep this darn place running. The heating costs were also immense due to the size of the house and the fact that the place was inadequately insulated. As my wife and children were at home all day and it was always around 25 degrees in the house, the heating drained the tanks in no time at all. I used around 12,000 litres of heating oil a year. An enormous cost factor.

But my dissatisfaction with my life grew steadily and constantly. After all, what good is all that money if you don't have a life to live?

Now more on the topic: You ruin your whole life with too much work

I loved my father-in-law very much. He was a great, simple, down-to-earth man. He was like a magnet that held the whole family together. We had a good relationship right from the start and he was more of a father to me than my biological father. If I needed advice, he always had an open ear for me. His advice was often simple and to the point.

What I always loved was his patriarchal manner: when a family get-together was called for, he wouldn't let anyone be absent. As I've always been a total family man, I was happy to follow my father's 'orders'. My parents-in-law lived in the Uckermark, in a very idyllic location on an ancient farm.

I loved it there because it reminded me of my childhood in the countryside. The farm was right next to a forest, with a view of a bend in the river - just great.

Like me, my father-in-law was a total workaholic. In his main job as a forester, he kept the farm going after work. Like me, he worked ten to twelve hours a day. He was very frugal and rarely went on holiday with my mother-in-law, and then only to the Baltic Sea or the Harz Mountains. It couldn't cost anything. My father-in-law never saw the rest of the world, even though he would have had the money for it. In short: just working, not living. Exactly the same life I'm living right now.

I lost this great father substitute to cancer in 2001. His death tore a hole in my life that I couldn't fill for a long time. He was not only like a father to me, but also my mentor, my support, my refuge when everything else fell apart at the seams. When he left, it felt like I had lost my compass.

I fell into a deep hole. The grief was overwhelming and suddenly all the things that used to drive me so much - work, success, status - were meaningless. His absence was like an echo in my everyday life, reminding me again and again how much of my life I had missed out on because I was constantly busy.

Here, for the first time, I had real doubts as to whether I wanted to continue my life in this form. All the hours I had spent in offices, on business trips or in meetings suddenly seemed like wasted time. What was it all for? For a full bank account? For a fatter car? For an ego that constantly craves validation?

I came to the conclusion that I urgently needed to change something. "Screw the money and start living," I thought to myself. But how do you put such a thought into practice when you've done nothing but plough for years? It was like trying to suddenly steer a heavy locomotive in the other direction. Difficult, but not impossible.

I decided to slow down, experience things more consciously and make time for my family and my young sons. Because his death had shown me in a brutal way that our lives are finite - and that the question of whether we have really lived our lives is more important in the end than any commission statement.

Life after death - is there really such a thing?

I was a believer, convinced that there must be something after death. In any case, I clung to this hope, because without it, life simply seemed meaningless to me.

In 2004, a major operation was scheduled: the removal of all four wisdom teeth. It was to be an outpatient operation under general anaesthetic. The room was cool, the air filled with the quiet hum of medical equipment. The anaesthetist leaned over me, his smile professional but distant. "I'm going to count to three, you're about to fall asleep," he said, his voice calm and controlled. I heard him counting and as soon as he had said the number three, the world around me seemed to dissolve.

The next moment was a mystery. A moment later - or so it felt to me - I was gently woken by a nurse. Her voice was warm as she said: "The operation is long over, you've made it." I blinked and searched for a clue in my complete disorientation. "When do we start?" I asked, confused. She laughed lightly and repeated that it was all over long ago.

The most amazing thing about this experience was not the physical recovery or the success of the operation. It was the feeling of absolute nothingness that pervaded me during the anaesthetic. No dream, no sense of time, no shadows of thought - just an all-encompassing darkness that began and ended without warning. "This is what death must be like," I thought to myself. An abrupt end in which the lights simply go out, and behind them there is silence. No continuation of life, no transition - just a hole, deep and silent.

This realisation made me shudder. If life only encompasses this limited period of time, a patchwork of obligations, work and the hunt for recognition, what remains? The death of my father-in-law, which still throbbed like a wound in my soul, suddenly came into sharper focus. His life, which consisted only of work and the constant en-deavour to provide for the family financially, appeared to me in all its tragedy. He had never known the happiness of simple *being* . He was the rock that carried everyone, but could never let go.

I swore to myself that I would not go down the same path. Life had to be more than just numbers, tables and the seemingly endless re-petition of the same processes. For the first time, I dared to think about what really mattered. Was it the smiles of my children, which I saw too rarely because I left the house before sunrise and only returned late at night?

I no longer wanted to be a shadow rushing through the days, driven by the fear of not being enough. Instead, I wanted to feel, live, breathe - do all the things that had always fallen short in my imagi-nation. And when the lights went out again one day, I didn't want to step into the darkness and regret that I had never really felt the glow of life.

So test he who binds himself forever...

I have no idea why I fell in love with her. Her nature was rather brittle and chilly, like a cold breeze on a winter's morning.

Emotional warmth was rarely felt, there was never any real depth. Nevertheless, she had her merits. What I had appreciated about her was her undeniable sense of beauty, her gift for creating a cosy home and her strong sense of family. These qualities attracted me at a time when I was looking for stability and structure. We met at a financial convention in the mid-nineties - one of those stiff events where the air is pregnant with ambitious conversations.

She was an impressive figure, a successful businesswoman with brunette hair, a slim figure and expressive, dark doe eyes that were hard to forget. Her smile was rare, but when it came, it was like a fleeting ray of sunshine through thick clouds. Her charisma was a mixture of elegance and coldness, and that fascinated me more than it should have at the time.

We quickly found a good connection with each other. It turned out that we didn't live far from each other, and so we met up again, which led to a relationship.

This relationship was like a blazing fire from the very beginning - hot and destructive at the same time. There were many break-ups, followed by the inevitable return. At the time, I thought it was passion. Opposites attract, I thought. It was only years later that I realised that what attracted us was also what separated us. In the long run, similarities matter more and everything else becomes a constant source of friction.

In 1997 we decided to get married. This decision caused a storm in my family. My parents were strictly against this marriage. Their disapproval went so far that they didn't come to the wedding reception or the wedding. The rest of my relatives were influenced by them and my sister and also stayed away. No phone calls, no congratulations, just silence, which weighed heavier than any arguments.

This rejection tore something inside me apart, and in my pride and disappointment I broke off contact. The break was final. My father died in 2017 without me ever speaking to him again... screw it.

Back to my wife: our first son was born in 1998 and I was prouder than words can describe. My heart was filled with a happiness that I had never known before. Our second son followed in 2001. Life felt like a perfectly orchestrated piece in those first few years - career, family, the newly purchased house near Berlin. Everything seemed to be in perfect order. But beneath the shiny surface, cracks began to appear.

With the birth of our children and life as a housewife, my wife began to change. She became more and more dotty and increasingly looked like a typical housewife who only looked after the home and hearth. Her once eloquent and quick-witted manner seemed to have disappeared. Instead, a narrow-mindedness emerged, coupled with a worrying lack of information.

This was particularly noticeable at business meetings, which I sometimes took her to. At first I thought she was just having a bad day, but it became more and more obvious - and, to be honest, more embarrassing - as time went on. She often made completely incoherent comments, was ill-prepared or seemed disinterested.

I noticed how my business partners looked at each other more and more questioningly and I sank inwardly with shame. It hurt me to see her like this, because this was not the woman I had once known. Her former sharp-witted and winning personality had been wiped away. Instead, I was left with the impression of a woman who had lost herself - and both of us along with her.

I was the one carrying the financial burden and my job was going extremely well, earning me 20,000 to 30,000 euros a month. She enjoyed this prosperity, I was convinced of that. The money was invested in the finest clothes, high-quality furnishings and expensive outings. The supply was always there, like an inexhaustible spring. But there was a lack of things that money couldn't buy: Closeness, tenderness, words like "I love you".

After the birth of our second child, intimacy also disappeared. There was no physical closeness for two years and every attempt on my part was blocked with a cold wall of silence. I searched for answers, wondering what had changed, but an open conversation was not possible.

The day that put my life on a completely wrong track

Then came that Sunday morning. We were sitting at the breakfast table, the children were playing in their rooms. I plucked up my courage and broached the subject: "Honey, I miss our closeness. It's as if there's nothing left between us. Do you think that's normal?"

Her answer hit me to the core.

"You sissy, pull yourself together. I'm not in the mood for you. Get over it."

I was shocked by the abysmal malice of this statement. I couldn't believe what she was like. It showed me that something was very wrong between us. I then sat quietly at the table for another hour without talking to her again. She took care of her household chores five metres away from me and didn't even look at me. She must have realised how I was feeling, but there was no apology or anything like that.

There I sat, the man who gave everything for his family, and heard that the woman I loved no longer felt anything for me.

I was numb for days afterwards and only spoke to her when I needed to. I waited for a sign of remorse, a word of regret. But nothing came. So I drew my conclusions.

I decided that our marriage was over inside, even if I was still there on the outside. This was the beginning of my descent into a world that fascinated me as much as it destroyed me. I registered on a dating site and quickly found women who gave me what I craved: reassurance, warmth, tenderness.

It wasn't long before the first ladies got in touch and the first dates were arranged. I met countless women over the next few months and I was amazed at how easy it was to get the ladies into bed. I wrote in the office in the morning, had a lunch date in the afternoon and then usually ended up in bed with the mouse a short time later. I had fun and sex without end. I could easily conceal it all as I was travelling a lot anyway and was also at "conferences" overnight. To be honest, it was a very, very cool time. However, it also had serious consequences, as the next chapters will show.

It also showed me that I was still attractive to other women as a man - exactly the feeling I no longer had with my wife.

My childhood in the GDR

Okay, my childhood was by and large normal. As normal as it could be in the former GDR. Despite imposed socialism and the supposed "equality of all people", society was deeply divided. The inequalities could be felt everywhere, a constant undertone in everyday life that divided people into three unequal classes.

The first class consisted of the Politburo commissars, the untouchables, the chosen ones of the system. They lived in secluded villas, protected behind high walls and guarded by security forces. Just think of the Honecker estate in Wandlitz, where the party elite enjoyed their privileges - swimming pools, imported food, medical care to Western standards. Their children went to special schools where they were spared the problems of ordinary life. They lived in their own, almost surreal world, in which the ideals of socialism merely served as a backdrop.

Then came the second class - the people who had relatives in the West and whose foreign currency gave them access to the "Inter-shops" . These shops, a mystery to us who only knew the shop windows, offered goods that the average GDR citizen could only dream of: Chocolate from Belgium, jeans from the USA, perfume from France. These people were the pinnacle of creation, and they showed it. You saw them in their shiny cars and with the latest achievements from the West - cassette recorders, branded clothes, nylon stockings. These people felt they were better than everyone else and looked down on the normal people with arrogance. At the disco, they wore their Levis jeans and were the biggest. I, on the other hand, stood there in my salt-and-pepper trousers made of cheap, ill-fitting flannel.

The message was clear: "Look what I have and what you will never have." This demonstrative superiority was a constant reminder that equality only existed on paper.

And then there was the third class, to which my family belonged. The class that had to make do with the grey reality of the economy of scarcity. We had no relatives in the West to provide us with parcels full of prosperity and the scent of freedom. Our shopping was a constant struggle. We stood in endless queues for hours, only to be told at the end that things were already sold out. The promise of socialism, equality and justice for all, was nothing but a hollow slogan. A system that preached to liberate people had in fact put us in invisible chains, trapped in a cage of deprivation.

But back to my mum. She always wanted to belong. She wanted to be part of the glittering second class, wanted to belong to those who walked past us with a smug smile while we pulled our thin jackets tighter and accepted the lack.

Why this wish? Perhaps because the neighbours to our left and right were second class. They drove western cars, which were sensational even in the GDR. One of our neighbours even drove a Mercedes - a symbol of luxury and a slap in the face to those who travelled in a Trabant or Wartburg, if they were lucky enough to own a car at all. Next to it was a Moto Guzzi motorbike, a magnificent specimen that magically attracted attention.

The guy loved to show off these symbols of his wealth. He deliberately left the vehicles outside so that anyone passing by could admire the precious possessions. It was as if he was saying to us: "You can dream of equality for a long time, but here I am, and I'm better than you." It was a display of arrogance that filled my young self with a mixture of admiration and anger. What a smug arsehole.

To understand this, you need to know what Genex was. Genex was a trading company, a channel between the worlds, through which citizens of the FRG could buy goods for their relatives in the East. Naturally at inflated prices that hardly anyone could afford. These goods - whether it was a pair of brand new Adidas shoes, coffee or a car - were then ceremoniously handed over to the East German relatives, who treated them like a treasure. And this neighbour, this guy, was living proof of how unfair the system was.

He shaped my childhood more than I realised at the time. His constant display of wealth fuelled my mother's insatiable desire to prove herself and keep up. She wanted to belong, whatever the cost.

She also wanted to have a "West car", wanted to experience the feeling of being part of this second class. There was an opportunity to buy a run-down Fiat model on the black market - for 150,000 East German marks, a price that was beyond all reason for a car that was barely worth DM 2,000 in the West. But this dream ate up our savings.

My mum always wanted to belong. This urge to join the glamorous world of those who had more, who above uswere , drove her to do all sorts of things. For her, a "West car" was more than just a means of transport - it was a symbol, a status symbol that was supposed to show: "Look, I'm no less than you." The car was her ticket to a club that, in her mind, was only open to the chosen ones.

It was a time when the pursuit of these symbols meant making sacrifices, and we did. The battered Fiat that my mother had bought on the black market swallowed up all our savings. 150,000 Ostmarks for a car that was barely worth DM 2,000 in the West. The figure alone was grotesque, but for my mother it was a price she was prepared to pay. The dream of recognition, of respect, had its price - and we all paid it too. Saving meant that there was only ever the cheapest food - and far too little of it. No wonder I weighed just 45 kilograms at the age of 16. We also saved on clothes: we only had the cheapest clothes, which neither fitted well nor were particularly stylish. I looked like a "Lui", as we used to say. Logically, I was often the target of ridicule and bullying because of my appearance. It was easy for the others to make fun of me - I was a real target.

The money that my father had earned in countless night shifts making furniture was put into this car. I remember the smell of sawdust and varnish that filled our house and the constant whirring of the home-made lathe.

The furniture was his masterpiece, lovingly crafted to keep us afloat. And although these pieces were a rarity and almost a treasure in the GDR's economy of scarcity, he never had the gleam in his eye that my mother had when the Fiat was finally parked in our driveway.

Man, was she proud. Proud like a queen in her kingdom, finally wearing her crown. The neighbour, who always set the tone, actually came over and spoke to her, if only a few fleeting words.

He gave her an appreciative nod, and at that moment everything was accomplished for her. The neighbour, who flaunted his chic Moto Guzzi and Mercedes like jewels, paid his respects. But this small triumph of my mum's had its price - and it was me who paid it.

With my meagre 45 kilos, I was an easy target for the strong ones at school. The bullying was relentless, the teasing painful, and the teachers looked the other way, as was so often the case in those days.

I sought shelter at home, but there was nothing but emptiness. My parents had no ear for my complaints. When I stood in front of them crying and asking for help, the answer was always the same: "Don't be like that, deal with it." So I learnt to keep quiet. I learnt to endure pain and hide my fear. I learnt that I was on my own.

There we see it: narcissists are devoid of empathy. They can't see beyond their own world, and my mum was the prime example of this. Her voice echoed through the house every day, shrill and demanding, accompanied by the hard slaps of her hand when she lost her temper. Hardly a day went by in my teenage years without her shouting at me or hitting me. Sometimes I thought she really hated me.

It was a cruel irony that I was bullied at school and found no safe haven at home. The house, which offered other children protection and warmth, was another place of horror for me. For the life of me, I can't remember when my mum ever gave me a hug or told me she loved me. Those words that should have come so easily from her lips remained trapped inside. It was different for my younger sister. She was the 'nestling' who could never be wrong. She was the shining centre around whom everything revolved.

Later, as an adult, this injustice continued. My parents favoured my sister's child, giving her love and attention that my children never knew. They went on holiday with my niece, while my children hardly knew what their grandparents looked like. No phone calls, no cards for birthdays or holidays - nothing. It was as if we didn't exist, and that gnawed at me, causing an anger to rise up in me that I could barely control.

My mum, I'm sure of it today, had psychological problems. Anyone who got too close to her and didn't conform to her ideas was banished from her life. Friends, neighbours, even family members - they all fell victim to her moodiness and her urge to control. My father, the gentle man who hid behind sawdust and wood shavings in the workshop, didn't have the strength to stand up to her. His silence was his protection, his attempt to in a marriage.survive

Sometimes I saw my mum hitting him, humiliating him, while he remained silent, his shoulders slightly slumped, his eyes on the floor.

He was a gentleman of the old school who would never have raised his hand to a woman, and I admired that. But it also made me angry. Because if he put up with it, it also meant that he didn't intervene when she hit me, when she hurt me. Maybe because he didn't know how to fight such an inner demon himself.

I learnt patience and manual dexterity from my father, but I also learnt what it means to live in the shadow of fear. I learnt how to remain silent to keep the peace and how to become invisible so as not to be a target. It was a lesson that shaped me - a lesson that I later found hard to shake off.

You are what has shaped you - never apologise for it.

Everything you have experienced, every pain, every happiness, every decision, has made you the person you are today. There is no need to justify yourself for your past. Your experiences, whether good or bad, are the cornerstone of your character, your strength and your uniqueness. They are as much a part of you as your name. So own up to what has shaped you and don't let anyone tell you that you have to apologise for it.

I think a lot of my behaviour and aggression came from the negative experiences of my childhood, bullying and unequal treatment. These formative years, in which I learnt that love is conditional and that protection remains an illusion, left scars that stayed with me for a long time. As an adult, I carried these scars around with me like an invisible weight, and ultimately many other negative experiences led me to break off contact with my parents and my sister.

A particularly formative moment was the wedding, which my parents ignored as if it were a casual side note in my life. It was as if they had drawn an invisible line under our relationship - except that this line had been there from the beginning, I had just never really seen it. But I'll come to that in a later chapter. The lack of understanding that had tormented me all those years grew into a bitter realisation: I didn't know what I had done wrong or why my parents never accepted me for who I was.

At some point, I had to realise that it wasn't me. My mum was not a normal woman. Her personality structure - narcissistic and manipulative - was like a net in which the people around her became entangled and wriggled helplessly. She played the cards of emotional abuse with a masterful perfection that only made me realise much later as an adult how sick the dynamic had really been. since I haven't exchanged a word with her and I never will again. Sometimes cuts are necessary to survive.2011

My father, the quiet hero of my childhood, died of dementia in 2019. It is an irony of life that the man who endured so much spent his last moments in a state in which he could probably hardly remember anything.

He died without me being allowed to see him again. My mother and sister, always anxious to maintain control, prevented my visit to the hospital. They cut me out like an unwanted footnote. I only found out about my father's death weeks later - via the probate court, as if it were incidental information in an administrative act. His ashes were scattered in an alpine meadow in Switzerland. This meant that there was no place I could go to say goodbye. No headstone, no flowers, just an emptiness that grew inside me.

This last chapter of alienation intensified my resentment and aggression. During this time, I felt betrayed by everything and everyone, even by my own story. What does something like that do to a person? It corrodes you from the inside. You start to question the value of all relationships. Does honesty even exist anymore? Are there real, deep and genuine feelings? If even those who fathered and raised you let you down, how can you trust anyone else?

From that point on, mistrust was my constant companion. Relationships that once had meaning became playgrounds of caution. I no longer allowed myself any deep feelings, forcing myself to keep my distance. It was a mechanism to avoid being hurt like before. Love became an act for me, a role I played because it was expected of me. **I imitated what love should look like**, showed what others wanted to see, but there was nothing behind it. Only emptiness.

The strange thing was that this distance, this subtle coldness that I radiated, attracted the women even more. It was as if my reserved behaviour was a riddle they wanted to solve, a fire they wanted to light. I enjoyed the attention, the admiration, the feeling of being desired, but they never got any closer to me. In the end, I only saw the people around me as a means of satisfying my needs at . Distance was my protective shield and I thought it was the only way to keep myself safe.

This is where the "lollipop effect" comes into play. If you're not familiar with it, here's a brief explanation: Imagine you hold out a lollipop to a child because you want to give it away. The child, defiant and stubborn, says "No". You take the lollipop back and casually say "Well, then don't", turn round and walk away. And what happens next? That's right - the child starts to cry, his little hand outstretched, and now wants the lollipop all the more.

This paradox of human desire is not only evident in children, but in many facets of life. Humans strive to possess that which eludes them, that which seems unattainable. This dynamic can be used as a subtle form of manipulation, whether consciously or unconsciously, and it works surprisingly well.

The paradox is that many people are more willing to walk ten kilometres backwards to find something lost than to walk a single kilometre forwards to gain something new.

This fact describes a deep, fundamental truth about human nature: the instinctive urge to win back what has been lost, even if the path to doing so is arduous and painful. And that was exactly what characterised me for a long time. The desire for recognition and clinging to what used to be paralysed me. But at some point I learnt to let go of these ghosts of the past.

In the end, it was good to exclude these people from my life. For many, kinship may be seen as an inviolable bond, a free pass for indulgence and forgiveness. But at some point I realised that this assumption was a fatal mistake. Blood may be thicker than water, but it is no guarantee of respect or humanity.

People who repeatedly hurt you, who break your trust and overshadow you don't deserve a place in your life - regardless of whether they are relatives or not. So I say to those people, "Fuck you." That may sound harsh, but it was a release. Saying goodbye to false loyalty was an act of survival.

However, the grief over the loss of my father remains an open chapter that still echoes inside me today. I can't really come to terms with this topic because so many questions remain unanswered. Am I a bad son? Should I have sought contact despite all the negative experiences and endless disappointments? Was it my duty to be the bridge, to keep the connection, even if it was me who was constantly being hurt? These questions gnaw at me like a silent poison that never quite goes away. These thoughts keep popping up, if I'm honest, pretty much every day. Nothing is crueler than unresolved conflicts with loved ones. They haunt you, tug at you, eat into your soul like a rusty nail. There is nothing harder than knowing that you may never get another chance to resolve things that needed to be said or done.

Therefore, take the opportunity to resolve your conflicts while people are still around. Talk, shout, cry, but sort it out. It may be unpleasant, it may hurt, but it is the only way to find peace - with yourself and with those who are important to you. Time is running out and when it does, all that remains is the stale feeling of regret. So take the first step before it's too late.

The Bible says: "You shall honour your father and mother." A simple sentence that weighs so heavily in its clarity. But what does honour mean if the respect is not reciprocal? I have rolled this question back and forth in my head, on sleepless nights and in moments of quiet self-reflection. So far, I have not found an answer that gives me peace. And perhaps I never will.

But in the end, it doesn't matter. Because time is running out, inexorably and mercilessly. The years have passed, and with them the chance to change things again. The reality is that I could never look my father in the eye again, and this thought tormented me for a long time. But I had to accept that every person dies alone in the end. We crumble to dust and in time we are all forgotten. At the latest when our children and grandchildren have also gone, the memory of us will be completely extinguished and everything that once made us special will be carried away by the flow of time.

There is something inevitable and sobering about this realisation. But it also harbours a kind of freedom: live your life while you have it and do it in such a way that in the end you don't regret what you did or didn't do. Life is meaningless if you look at it through the eyes of eternity. You will find out why this is the case in the next chapter.

Men and their fathers - The generational conflict

As I said, my father was a very hard-working and talented man. I was always impressed by his calm manner. No matter what he tackled - it just worked. He was someone who never made a big fuss about his abilities, but his skills spoke for themselves. I remember how he bought an old, dilapidated house that others would have given up on long ago. But for him it was a challenge that he took on with dedication. He repaired the house piece by piece - no easy endeavour in the former GDR, where building materials were often in short supply. But my father always found a way.

He was an engineer by profession, and his ability to read and implement technical plans not only helped him to plan the construction. They also enabled him to barter for materials that were otherwise hard to come by. He traded his knowledge for what he needed and so the project began to take shape.

When I was a teenager, a new phase of our relationship began. We started building furniture together. He had built himself a wood-turning machine - another example of his creative craftsmanship and inventiveness.

This machine was impressive, and he used it to produce beautiful pieces of furniture that seemed almost like a small miracle in the GDR, where shortages were omnipresent. Furniture of this quality could not simply be bought. And so my father sold some of the pieces for good money - they were real rarities.

I definitely inherited my craftsmanship from him. Those hours we spent together in the workshop are still a valuable treasure for me today. The smell of wood, the whirring of the machine, the moments when I could look over his shoulder - those were moments when I was proud to be his son. It felt like he was teaching me something unique, something that not everyone could learn.

Another example was my first moped, and it is one of the fondest memories I have of my father. I was 14 years old when he said one day: "Come and see Grandad." My grandad lived a few houses away, in a large yard with a huge garage. My father led me into the garage, went to an old shelf and pulled out two huge, dusty boxes. "What's this?" I asked curiously. He opened the boxes and inside, dismantled into countless individual parts, was a moped - a complete **SR2**, a model from the 1960s.

He grinned and said: "Son, this will be our next project and I'll teach you how to drive." I could hardly believe it. A moped of my own! From then on, we were a team. We took out all the parts, sandblasted them carefully and painted them a shimmering blue-grey. Every part was inspected, every broken part repaired or replaced. We even took the engine apart. The whole thing took weeks, because we always worked on it after work - whenever my father had time.

One day, in the middle of summer, the time had come. The moped was finally ready. We filled it with petrol, pressed the carburettor three times and kick-started it. After the third attempt, the engine actually started. It was a magical moment. The old engine rattled as if it had just been waiting to be brought back to life. My father let it idle for a few minutes and then turned off the tap. "Son," he said, "we're going to push this thing into the woods now."

As I didn't have a driving licence, of course, we pushed the bike the 500 metres to the edge of the forest. Once there, on a forest path, he showed me how everything worked. I sat on the SR2 and my father explained the manual gearstick, which looked like a brake lever. "You pull the lever, turn the handle down for first gear, slowly release the clutch and accelerate. And then - off you go!"

With a pounding heart, I did everything exactly as he had explained. And sure enough, the moped started moving. **I was riding a moped for the first time in my life!** My God, that was an awesome feeling! I rode along the forest track, slowly, while my father ran alongside me and shouted instructions. After about 400 metres, I stopped and he showed me how to change to the next gear. Then he encouraged me to keep going and I did a few laps of the forest track.

That went on for two hours. **The best two hours of my life.** It wasn't just the driving, but the shared experience with my father that made this day so unforgettable. One of the few memories I still have of him so clearly today. It was a moment of pure joy and it felt like we owned the world.

But although I learnt a lot from him - how to solve problems, how to create something with your own hands that lasts - there was also something I missed.

My father was a master craftsman, but when it came to teaching me how to become a man, he meoften left alone. His calm manner, which I always admired, also showed its dark side here. There were rarely any conversations about life, about the challenges I had to overcome as a young man. It would certainly have helped me to receive more "wisdom" from a father here. Sometimes I wished he had explained to me what it means to be a man, how to behave in difficult situations or how to deal with my own feelings - things that are beyond the workshop and the blueprint.

Instead, his approach was often a wordless role model. He modelled what it meant to be hardworking, consistent and calm. He showed me how to tackle problems, but he rarely talked about them. Maybe it was just his way. Maybe he thought that I would learn by observing, that his example would be enough to show me the way. But as a young man looking for his own place in the world, I sometimes wished for more - more direct words, more guidance when it came to navigating life's uncertainties.

Looking back, I understand better why he was the way he was. He himself grew up in a time and under circumstances where men rarely talked about feelings or personal challenges. It was about survival, about getting things done, and feelings were often pushed aside because there was no room for them. But in my youth, when I was trying to figure out how to assert myself as a man in the world, I sometimes felt left alone. Craftsmanship was valuable - and I'm grateful for it. But how to deal with the pressures of life, how to be strong and vulnerable as a man at the same time, was something I had to painstakingly work out for myself.

It's not that I blame him. In many ways, I still admire my father today - for his ability to find solutions in a difficult time, for his patience and his diligence. But I believe that many men in my generation have had similar experiences. We often learnt practical skills from our fathers, but the emotional side of masculinity was often left unspoken. We had to for ourselvesfigure out how to navigate as men in a world that is constantly changing.

Maybe that's one of the reasons why I think about these things so often during the menopause. I wonder what I was like as a father, whether I did it better. Have I shown my children not only how to fix things or solve problems, but also how to deal with insecurities and fears? Have I created the emotional connection that I often lacked myself? These questions stay with me, because while I am grateful to my father in many ways, I also know that being a man today requires more than just manual dexterity and perseverance.

I have four sons and it was always important to me to avoid my own father's mistakes when bringing them up. I didn't just want to be the silent observer, but an active counsellor, someone they could come to when they needed advice. Anyone who has sons my age knows how rebellious they can be - especially in adolescence when they are trying to find their own identity and rebelling against what they perceive as parental control.

But it was precisely at these moments that it was important for me to show a different kind of leadership. I never used violence in my parenting. It was not a way for me to gain respect or build a connection with my sons. Instead, I always tried to show them that there were other ways to solve a problem - ways based on reason and dialogue, not coercion.

Of course, as with all parenting, there were moments when consequences were necessary. If they refused to listen or deliberately went against what I was trying to teach them, I had to set boundaries. But I always chose the path of depriving them of something that was important to them instead of using force.

This often worked wonders. When the mobile phone or PlayStation was suddenly no longer there and they had to do without their favourite games for a while, they quickly realised that their actions had consequences. Or when I secured the motorbike with a lock and they were not allowed to use it, they realised that their freedom could not be taken for granted. Pocket money was also an effective way of teaching them responsibility.

It wasn't a punishment in the traditional sense, but a lesson: decisions have consequences, and sometimes you have to pay the price if you make the wrong choices.

I could put countless anecdotes on paper. There were moments when I was secretly amused by their creative attempts to circumvent the rules, but ultimately these small battles were part of the larger process of moulding them into responsible young men. With imagination, I think everyone can form their own picture of these situations. The fights for the last word, the negotiations about going out and the countless times they tried to convince me with their arguments are unforgettable.

But in hindsight, I realise that all these arguments were valuable. They taught them that life doesn't always go your way and that you have to stick to the rules, even if they sometimes seem unreasonable.

At the end of the day, I was lucky. My sons have all turned out well. Not only did they work hard at school, but they also proved in their apprenticeships that they are prepared to take on responsibility. All four of them have completed a decent education and now have a permanent job. This is not a matter of course in a world that is constantly changing and in which competition is becoming tougher.

My partner and I were lucky enough to live on the outskirts of the city, where our children could grow up sheltered, far away from the problems and influences that might have been different in some neighbourhoods. They never came into contact with criminal chaos, as you sometimes hear in the news, and I am grateful for that. Of course, you can never rule out all risks in life, but I think our environment has helped them develop into the responsible young men they are today.

Sometimes I think about how different my sons' lives would have been if they had grown up in a less sheltered environment. But ultimately it wasn't just the environment that made the difference - it was also the way we as parents responded to their needs.

My ex-wives and I tried to always be present, always listen and at the same time give them the space to make their own mistakes. It wasn't always easy, because there's this fine line between letting go and holding on, which you have to balance every day as a father. But I think we have mastered this fine line quite well.

It's a strange feeling to look back now and see how the little boys who once took their first steps have become grown men. Men who go their own way, who make their own decisions and - I hope - apply some of the lessons I taught them in their lives. Of course, I am aware that they will not always act according to my ideas. But that's okay. After all, I didn't teach them to blindly follow my path, but to find their own way - and I'm proud of that.

Meep-Meep-Meep -the Roadrunner-

In 2022, I had an appointment with a urologist. My wife had arranged it; I had resisted an examination for years because I had a certain sense of shame. The mere thought of another man fumbling around in my bum made my hair stand on end every time. This feeling, this deep-rooted aversion, was more than just shame - it was a mixture of pride and a kind of illogical defiance. As if, by avoiding this visit, I could maintain control over my own integrity.

"Are you still in your right mind?" my wife asked me when I told her my motives. Her voice was a mixture of impatience and concern, the kind of tone that only someone who really loves and cares can adopt. "You men are really crazy. Would you rather get cancer?" There it was, the awkward moment of truth. Getting cancer would undoubtedly be the worst-case scenario. Her objection made me pause for a moment. The thought of jeopardising my life through my pride was absurd. So I agreed, but on the day of the appointment, I walked into the surgery with a heavy heart - as if I was entering a battlefield.

The practice was modern, the air filled with the typical odour of disinfectant coming from one of those little plastic dispensers that nobody takes seriously. The walls were painted a calming blue, as if the colour was supposed to ease my inner tension. The examination itself was unpleasant, but nowhere near as bad as I had imagined. The doctor, a middle-aged man with friendly eyes and an unobtrusive smile, asked me how I was feeling.

"Oh, well, everything's fine," I said, trying to sound as relaxed as possible. A wry grin appeared on his face and he replied: "You're the first man of your age to say something like that." It was at this moment that I discovered a spark of humour that I hadn't expected.

"Really?" I asked with a short laugh that masked my own nervousness.

"I'm your doctor and, like your dentist, I can only help you if you open your mouth," he said dryly and with a twinkle in his eye. The sentence was so unexpected that I had to laugh. The ice was broken and suddenly I felt like I could finally talk.

It gushed out of me like water from an old, rusty pipe that had been closed for too long. I talked about the last few months, the mood swings, the feeling of restlessness that plagued me and the shadows that had spread through my psyche. I also talked about the creeping sexual reluctance that had been driven like an invisible wedge between my wife and me. The doctor nodded sympathetically and asked specific questions that made me feel like I was being taken seriously. It was as if a weight had been lifted from my shoulders.

After this initial, unfamiliar openness, he suggested hormone treatment. He patiently explained that an imbalance in testosterone levels can have not only physical but also psychological effects. I agreed to a blood test and the first hurdle was overcome. Three weeks later, I was back at his practice , this time with a certain anxiety consisting of a mixture of curiosity and fear.

"Your testosterone level is 3.0 nmol/l," he said as he spread the lab sheet out on his desk. The normal range is between 12 and 35 nmol/litre. That explained a lot - the tiredness, the constant irritability, the feeling that my body and mind were no longer synchronised. The doctor suggested a testosterone treatment with the preparation Nebido and explained to me how it would work and what possible side effects could occur.

"It's up to you," said the doctor, "but I don't think you'll regret it."

He immediately gave me the prescription and I went straight to the pharmacy and then back to the surgery with the testosterone. The doctor looked at me with a scrutinising look, as if he had doubts as to whether I was really ready for this step. He wanted to postpone the appointment to make sure we weren't rushing into anything. But I didn't let up, insisting on doing it straight away. The hope that all my problems would finally vanish into thin air was stronger than any caution.

No sooner said than done - the syringe in my arse and then off home. I was curious, almost excited, but the real surprise didn't come until the next morning.

I woke up as if someone had flicked a lever in my head. An unfamiliar, almost electric energy flooded my body. It felt like I had woken up from a long, dark sleep. The first thought that popped into my head was: "Meep, meep, the roadrunner is on his way." A smile spread across my face that I hadn't felt in years. It was more than just energy - it was pure lust for life, as if someone had rekindled the embers inside me.

This feeling intensified even further over the next few days. An inner warmth flowed through my body, like a gentle current that vibrated my muscles, my skin and my entire organism. It was as if I had reached into a socket and was suddenly connected to the network of life. The blood pulsed with a vigour that I had long thought lost, and it spurred me on to finally become active again.

I grabbed my sports kit, which had been gathering dust for the last few months, and headed to the gym. Once there, I immediately realised that this day was going to be different.

The usual routine suddenly felt easy, almost effortless. On the bench press, where I normally struggled with 80kg, that day I lifted 110kg with ease. It was as if the Hulk himself had taken over my body. I'm not exaggerating when I say that the effect of the prescription testosterone was drastic and noticeable.

Unlike my first Testo treatment with the Poland test agoa few years , which I now realised was obviously inferior, this new treatment was pure and powerful. The increase in strength was not only physical, but also mental. The doubts that had accompanied me for years seemed to dissolve in the light of this new-found vitality.

The side effects were also not as extreme as with the adulterated Polish testo that I had tried years ago. Back then, I was always struggling with sudden outbreaks of sweating, a racing heart and uncontrollable irritability. But this time it was different. Sure, the effect was strong, almost frighteningly strong, but it came without the feeling that my body was working against me. It was as if I had regained control - as if my body was finally my ally and no longer my opponent.

And now? Now the punk really took off. This new energy was more than just a physical phenomenon. It was like a spark that awakened my spirits and shook me out of years of lethargy. Everything felt more intense, more alive. I could feel how my view of the world changed, how the grey veil that had covered my thoughts slowly disappeared. I felt like the man I always wanted to be: strong, self-confident, ready to face life's challenges with my head held high.

A few years earlier, in 2008, I had already had my first experience with a testosterone programme. At the time, I was tired of looking like an asparagus tarzan with my lean 55 kg.

The urge to finally appear strong and confident had become overpowering. I no longer wanted to be the guy who was always overlooked, but someone who attracted attention, a man who stood out in the room and commanded respect.

The trigger for this decision was a meeting with an old friend I hadn't seen for a long time. When he walked in the door, I could hardly believe my eyes: where a slim, unassuming used to nerd stand, there was now a 105kg muscleman who looked like he had drunk straight from a comic of Miraculix's magic potion.

I wanted to look like that too. I wanted to finally feel like a 'real' man and, last but not least, be more popular with the ladies.

No sooner said than done: I travelled to Poland with a friend, where at the Polish market almost everything was available . Between stalls selling leather jackets and cheap electronic devices, I bought my first testosterone syringes. Back home, the moment of truth arrived: out with the syringe, in with the arse. It takes a lot of effort to inject yourself, but that didn't stop me. Luckily, I was always someone who had no problems with visits to the dentist, injections and blood tests. I remember my mum being amused by how "cool" I was as a little toddler during visits to the doctor, while other children ran away screaming or crying. I sat calmly in my chair and let everything happen to me. This calmness was now paying off.in Slubice

The day after the first injection, I went to the gym with renewed vigour. My anticipation was already boiling on the way there. I was determined to turn the tables and counter the sardonic looks of the other guys who had smiled at me until then. "You bastards, you'll see what happens now," I thought to myself as I entered the studio. It was an inner mantra that drove me to perform at my best over the coming weeks. I trained like a maniac every day, filling my body with protein shakes and piling up plates full of meat and rice. The days passed in a frenzy of sweat, sore muscles and the satisfied feeling that something was finally changing.

After just 30 days, the results were clear to see. I had reached almost 80kg and was full of energy. Those around me were amazed, and even my wife at the time, who was usually rather reserved with compliments, couldn't help but nod appreciatively.

The physical change also brought about other changes: I felt full of life, had more self-confidence than ever before and was full of drive - also in terms of sexuality. I was constantly recharged, always ready, always hungry for more.

The testosterone programme lasted six weeks and afterwards I felt like a new person. I maintained my weight and muscle mass and continued to train in the years that followed. In my heyday, I weighed a proud 107 kg at a height of 175 cm. Today, many years later, I still weigh a solid 93 kg.

But at the beginning of 2019, the dark side of the story returned. My mood swings became more extreme, I was irritable, impatient and often found myself in moments where everything and everyone got on my nerves. The familiar tension and emotional ups and downs reminded me of the time before my first testosterone treatment. I thought back to 2008 and decided to give it another go - but this time in a legal and safe way. The thought of travelling to Poland again and getting the syringes on the black market now seemed foolish and dangerous.

Because there is one thing you need to know: Deca-Durabolin and similar products that can be bought cheaply on Polish markets may be tempting, but their quality and origin are often questionable. The ampoules could contain anything from impurities to harmful substances that harbour potentially fatal risks. It was now clear to me that anyone who gambles with their health is risking more than just their reputation. That's why my advice is: stay away from polish.

If the book is too crass or offensive in places, I apologise. It was never my intention to hurt anyone or cause offence. My aim was to describe my experiences at the time as authentically as possible - raw, honest and unfiltered, as I felt them at the time. This also includes a somewhat coarse slang that some would describe as "Berlin redneck big mouth". This way of expressing myself is part of my background, it is direct, blunt and sometimes harsh.

I decided to keep this tone because I think it best conveys what I've been through. The feelings, the anger, the hurt - you can't always put all that into soft words. It wouldn't be real. In a life that is often full of complexity and contrasts, this direct language was reflected and it helped me to organise and process my emotions.

So if some passages seem too blunt or provocative, I ask for your understanding. Sometimes life is not just black and white, but loud, unruly and unembellished. It is important to me to tell the truth of my own story as I experienced it - not to shock, but to be honest. And sometimes that requires a bit more rough edges.

How does testosterone production work in the male body?

Testosterone production in the male body is a complex process that mainly takes place in the testicles. Here are the most important aspects:

Production location and quantity

Around 90% of testosterone is produced in the Leydig cells of the testicles. The remaining 10% is produced in the adrenal glands. The starting material for testosterone biosynthesis is cholesterol.

Hormonal control

Testosterone production is controlled by the interaction of several hormones:

1. Gonadotropin-releasing hormone (GnRH): Released by the hypothalamus.

2. Luteinising hormone (LH): Released by the pituitary gland in response to GnRH.

3. Follicle stimulating hormone (FSH): Also produced by the pituitary gland.

LH stimulates the Leydig cells to produce testosterone, while FSH, together with testosterone, is responsible for sperm production.

Negative feedback

Testosterone regulates its own production through a negative feed-back mechanism. A high testosterone level inhibits the release of

GnRH in the hypothalamus and LH in the pituitary gland, which in turn reduces testosterone production.

Biosynthesis

Testosterone biosynthesis takes place in several steps:

1. Cholesterol is converted to pregnenolone.

2. Androstenedione is produced via various intermediate steps.

3. The enzyme testosterone-17β-dehydrogenase catalyses the final step from androstenedione to testosterone.

Transport and effect

After production, testosterone is released into the blood and transported to the target organs. It is largely bound to proteins such as sex hormone-binding globulin (SHBG) and albumin. Only about 1-2% of testosterone circulates freely in the blood. In the target tissues, part of the testosterone is converted into the even more effective dihydrotestosterone (DHT) by the enzyme 5α-reductase.

Testosterone production and effect varies throughout life. It begins during embryonic development, rises sharply during puberty and remains relatively stable in adulthood before slowly declining in old age.

How can a man boost his body's own testosterone production?

There are many natural ways to boost testosterone levels without resorting to drugs or hormone replacement therapies. Here are some of the best approaches:

---

1. sport and exercise

Regular physical activity is one of the most effective ways to stimulate testosterone production:

- **Interval training:** A combination of intensive and quiet training phases, such as HIIT (High-Intensity Interval Training), can increase testosterone levels by up to 40%. Just 20 minutes, three times a week, is sufficient.

- **Strength training:** Focus on exercises for large muscle groups (e.g. squats, deadlifts, bench presses) with short breaks. This stimulates testosterone production particularly effectively.

- **Balanced training:** Training too much or for too long can be counterproductive and increase cortisol levels, which inhibits the release of testosterone. A mix of strength and endurance training is ideal.

---

2. nutrition

A conscious diet can also help to improve testosterone levels in a natural way:

- **Oat flakes:** .They contain avenacosides, which promote the conversion of inactive testosterone precursors into biologically active testosterone

- **Green vegetables:** Broccoli, kale and spinach provide indole-3-carbinol, which inhibits the conversion of testosterone into oestrogen.

- **Healthy fats:** Unsaturated fatty acids from nuts, almonds, hemp oil or safflower oil are essential for hormone production.

- **Zinc-containing foods:** Zinc is a key nutrient for testosterone production and is found in foods such as oysters, pumpkin seeds and beef.

3. lifestyle adjustments

A healthy lifestyle is crucial for maintaining testosterone production:

- **Stress reduction:** Chronic stress increases the cortisol level, which blocks testosterone production. Yoga, meditation or regular time-outs can help.

- **Sufficient sleep:** The majority of testosterone is produced during deep sleep. 7-9 hours of sleep per night is ideal.

- **Weight management:** Excessive abdominal fat promotes the conversion of testosterone into oestrogen, which disrupts the hormone balance.

- **Intermittent fasting:** Fasting phases, especially in the evening, can have a positive effect on morning testosterone levels.

4. food supplements

Supplements can also help:

- **Vitamin D:** A deficiency of this "sun vitamin" can lead to lower testosterone levels. Supplementation is often particularly useful in winter.

- **Ashwagandha:** A herbal adaptogen that reduces stress and has been shown to increase testosterone production.

- **Zinc and magnesium:** Both minerals are essential for hormone production and are often contained in multivitamin supplements.

5. avoidance of pollutants

Chemicals from plastics can have a negative effect on hormone levels:

- **Reduce plastic products:** Phthalates and bisphenol-A (BPA), which are contained in many plastic products, act like artificial oestrogens and lower testosterone levels.

- **Favour natural materials:** glass, stainless steel or BPA-free alternatives are the better choice here.

Honey, I think I have a fever

It was 2019, the last holiday abroad before the Covid-19 pandemic. A holiday that began as normally as many before it, but would later turn out to be another building block in my personal story of self-discovery. The day got off to a great start: We were off to Antalya, into the sunshine that called to us as tantalisingly as a promise of relaxation and freedom. The early flight, scheduled at 08:00, meant that we still had the whole day ahead of us to explore the hotel, enjoy our first drink by the pool and take a deep breath that life was good right now.

The alarm clock rang at dawn and we got up early, accompanied by the pleasant excitement that only the start of a holiday can bring. The suitcase was already packed in the hallway, ready for the next adventure. We had a leisurely breakfast, sipped our coffee, exchanged a few plans for the first few days and savoured the tingle of anticipation. At 06:00 on the dot, the doorbell rang and our son, who had kindly offered to be our chauffeur, was at the door. BER, that huge, unloved airport, was only a 15-minute drive away and the roads were still quiet.

After the usual check-in procedure, which is always a mixture of patience and annoyed eye-rolling, we still had plenty of time before our departure. So we sat down in an airport café, ordered a cappuccino and watched the travellers around us as they hurried past with wheeled suitcases or drowsily sipped their drinks. Everything was fine. Until suddenly a strange feeling came over me. Without warning, I was overcome by a wave of heat, as if someone had flikked a switch and turned the heating in my body on full blast. My shirt was sticking to my back, beads of sweat were forming on my forehead and my mind was racing. "Oh dear, please not now, I want to go on holiday," I thought in a panic.

I turned to my wife and mumbled, "Honey, I think I have a fever." The expression on her face changed from concern to amused disbelief. She put her hand on my forehead, smiled broadly and said, "Honey, it's not a fever, you have a flush."

It has to be said that my wife is a nurse. She has a medical knowledge that is second to none at times like this, and then there's her dry sense of humour. "Flush? What kind of flush?" I was completely confused. The idea that men could have something like flushes was completely alien to me until that moment.

She grinned and said, "You always make fun of me when I say I have a flush. Well, darling, welcome to the club. You're going through the menopause." It was like someone had pulled the rug out from under my feet. All I could think was: "Oh dear... Am I slowly becoming an old dodderer now?"

On the plane, after my panic had subsided and the air conditioning had cooled me down halfway, my wife looked up a medical article on her mobile phone about the male menopause. I started reading, sceptically, but the further I got, the more I recognised the symptoms: Tiredness, irritability, mood swings and those darn heat waves. There was no mistaking it - this fine gentleman was now officially going through the menopause.

In the following months, the flushes occurred sporadically, like uninvited guests who simply drop by to make themselves known and then disappear again. These sudden bouts of heat are more than just unpleasant. They are like an invisible furnace being lit inside you, making everything inside you glow. The good news is that they pass after a few minutes, but those minutes feel like an eternity.

The flushes continue to this day, but the intervals have become longer. Over time, I have learnt to deal with them and accept them as part of this new chapter in my life. My wife, who still struggles with her own experience from time to time, can't help but smile when she realises that I've had it again. She then says with a twinkle in her eye: "Well, my dear, who has the last word now?" And despite everything, I still have to smile.

Then she always grins broadly: "Well, pufferfish, have you got a fever again? Should I go to the chemist?" A real doofus, my sweetie, but her jokes always lighten the mood. These little bits of banter are part of our dynamic, which always makes us laugh, even in the grey moments of everyday life. And yes, we have pet names for each other that would probably make outsiders shake their heads, but for us they are pure love. She is my "snail" and I am her "puffer fish".

Why "Schneckchen"? The name has its roots in a story that is so typical of us that I always like to tell it. My wife has a habit of surprising me with spontaneous sex interludes from time to time. Without warning, completely uninhibited - and regardless of what I'm doing.

Once I was in my home office, engrossed in an endless team meeting with colleagues who were all making important faces and making their points in serious voices. And suddenly, out of nowhere, she stood naked in the doorway, her eyes flashing mischievously, and without hesitation she came towards me. My heart skipped a beat and I had to mobilise everything in me to switch off the camera and microphone in time before the meeting took an unexpected turn. I suddenly didn't care about the chat or the meeting at all - my "Nacktschnegge" was there. The name was born and stuck, a little insider that always brings a smile to our faces when it comes up.

And why "puffer fish"? This story takes us back to one of our best holidays, in Antalya. It was a hot summer's day and we decided to visit the city's aquarium - a break from the sun and a chance to experience something new. We were strolling through the corridors, looking at the exotic fish, when we stopped in front of a tank with a particularly curious inhabitant: a fat, round puffer fish that stared at us with its beady eyes. She looked at me, smiled and said: "It looks just like you, copy it."

So I puffed out my cheeks, puffed out my belly and pulled a face that was so funny she burst out laughing. It was that honest, uninhibited laughter that makes you realise someone is genuinely amused from the heart. Her eyes started to water and she held her stomach as she almost fell to her knees laughing. The people around us, who had been looking on curiously at first, started laughing along, and suddenly the whole aquarium was filled with happy giggles and laughter - triggered by us two crazy Berliners who didn't give a damn what others thought of them. That was the moment I got rid of my nickname "puffer fish".

Since then, "Kugelfisch" has not only been a funny name, but a re-minder of how much joy we can give each other, even in the most banal moments. It's a sign of our carefree, silly love that accompa-nies us through thick and thin - whether it's laughing together on holiday or winking when I'm sweating like a marathon runner and she lovingly says to me: "Well, pufferfish, is it getting hot again?"

But back to the topic of hot flushes. The experience of having hot flushes as a man is not only surprising, but also confusing and so-metimes embarrassing. It feels like being intothrown a cycle that was previously completely unknown to you - and in my case, I initially thought that only women experienced this. But I had to learn that nature has its own plan and the menopause doesn't stop at men either.

So what are the main mechanisms that trigger these hot flushes? Here is a closer look:

1. **Decrease in testosterone levels**: Testosterone is the pri-mary male sex hormone, and it not only influences physical performance and libido, but also general well-being. As we age, production gradually decreases, leading to an imba-lance in hormone levels. This imbalance can cause a variety of symptoms, including the dreaded hot flushes. It's as if the

body is trying to adjust to new rules of the game that don't suit it.

2. **Changes in the hypothalamus**: The hypothalamus is like the body's thermostat. It ensures that the body temperature always remains in balance. However, if the hormones get out of sync, the hypothalamus can become irritated and send the wrong signals. It can falsely assume that the body is overheated and trigger a cascade of reactions: Blood vessels dilate, sweat breaks out, and the body desperately tries to get rid of the supposed heat. The result is a hot flush that hits you with an unpleasant force.

3. **Disruption of the autonomic nervous system**: The autonomic nervous system is like an autopilot for many of our involuntary bodily functions - heartbeat, breathing and even temperature regulation. If the hormone balance is disrupted, the autonomic nervous system can also be affected. Such a disruption can trigger an uncontrolled release of adrenaline and noradrenaline, which in turn the typical hot flushes atresults in . It feels as if the body switches to fight-or-flight mode without warning.

4. **Psychological and emotional factors**: Stress, anxiety and depression can act as catalysts for physical reactions. Particularly at a stage in life when men are often struggling with professional and personal pressures, these psychological stresses act as an accelerant on the body's physiological reactions. The hormones go crazy and the body responds with hot flushes that appear out of nowhere and leave behind a creeping restlessness.

5. **Medication use and health conditions**: An often overlooked factor is medication that suppresses testosterone production, for example in the treatment of prostate cancer. These drugs can trigger hot flushes as a side effect. However, other health problems such as obesity, diabetes and thyroid disorders also increase the risk. The body is a highly

complex system and if one component gets out of balance, this can have far-reaching consequences.

Almost all of these factors applied to me at the time. It felt like my body was developing a life of its own, one that I could no longer control. The hot flushes often came without warning, making me sweat in the middle of a meeting or waking me up at night when I was soaking wet in the sheets. Sometimes it felt like I had lost control of my own body and it was eating away at my self-image.

Beam me Back in 80s - Memories of the best time of my life

Let's talk about a difficult topic: mood swings, especially depression. Anyone who knows me knows that I have led a very eventful life, full of highs and lows, full of glamour and darkness. Even in the GDR, I wasn't the type to stand still. I was always on the move, looking for ways to make the best of my situation. Sewing was my craft back then and I made a good living from it. It was a time when creativity and hard work counted more than anything else, and I capitalised on that. From 1989 to 1991, I worked as a pastry chef at the Grand-hotel, one of the most prestigious addresses in the city, where the air smelled of sugar. It was a job that not only gave me manual skills, but also access to special privileges.

One such privilege was that I received part of my salary in West Marks - 100 West Marks per month, which were like a treasure in the GDR. These West Marks opened doors that remained closed to others. I could use this money to go shopping in the Intershops, shops that stocked goods from the capitalist West: the finest choco-late, real jeans, perfume. Things that ordinary people only knew from stories. If you didn't fancy Intershops, you could exchange your West German money for East German marks on the black market. The exchange rate was astronomical - 10 Westmarks fetched up to 300 Ostmarks. It was like Monopoly money that gave me access to a better world.

I always had my pockets full of money and lived the life that many people dreamed of. After work, I would sit in the best restaurants in the city. The Nicolai district with its historic alleyways was my second living room, the Palast der Republik my playground, the Operncafé my favourite disco. I had the Hotel Stadt Berlin and the Mokka-Milch ice cream bargreat times at.

My life changed radically in 1991. I was approached by sales people on the street and started a career at an insurance company that would turn my life upside down.

From , 1992I was earning no less than 20,000 Deutschmarks a month. The 100 West German marks from the GDR era were suddenly a piece of cake. The years that followed were a wild ride. If you've seen "The Wolf of Wall Street", you'll get the picture: I was just that kind of guy - only even more extreme. My lifestyle was a permanent adrenaline rush, a party that never ended. Parties, women, fast cars and the constant rush of money characterised my everyday life. It was a dance on the razor's edge, and back then I was convinced I was invincible. But the dark side of my lifestyle, which I ignored, would one day catch up with me.

In 2006, I decided to turn my back on the financial sector and concentrate solely on selling property. It was the right decision, because the property market was booming. I was earning well, living the high life and had more money than I could spend. My life was an endless stream of travelling, expensive restaurants and luxury hotels. At the same time, I was juggling three or four mistresses alongside my wife - a balancing act that couldn't go well in the long term.

Then came the turning point in 2007. I separated from my first wife, gave up my family, my life, my house and luxury for another woman.

It was a mistake that sent my life into a downward spiral. The hardest hit were my young sons, who felt the true tragedy of this decision. Shortly after the separation, I wanted to undo everything and realised that I had made an irreparable mistake, but it was too late. A bitter war of the roses began, which in the end cost me everything - not only emotionally, but also financially.

Personal insolvency loomed on the horizon like a looming storm with no escape. The loss of my broker's licence, the basis of my professional livelihood, was the ultimate consequence. I could no longer work without my business licence. In Germany, a real estate agent needs a clean slate, a flawless financial history, in order to keep his licence. And me? I was suddenly faced with the ruins of my life's work, watching everything I had built up disintegrate before my eyes.

The combination of professional ruin, the destruction of my family and the feeling of failure set a process in motion that I couldn't control at the time: deep mood swings and a depression that haunted me like an uninvited guest.

In 2010, I tried to get back on my feet with new business ideas, which I somewhat succeeded in doing. The years of upheaval and the search for stability challenged me in a way I had never experienced before. I threw myself into trading commodities, especially waste products and oil. It wasn't a glamorous business, but it had potential. The start was bumpy, as so often with new ventures, but I managed to make some income - nowhere near the astronomical amounts of before, but still 9 to 15K euros a month. That was enough to secure my livelihood and maintain my belief in my entrepreneurial ability.

Nevertheless, success felt hollow. The many wrong decisions of the past clung to me like an invisible shadow. At the age of 50, I began to realise that, despite all my efforts and struggles, I had nothing to show for it. No impressive investments, no solid pension cushion. My self-employment was barely keeping me afloat, but it wasn't what I had once dreamed of. The dreams of the past had faded, like pictures that had hung in the sun for too long. I struggled anew every month, and the prospect of growing old in an insecure financial situation gnawed at me.

The memories of better times haunted me like ghosts that wouldn't leave me alone. I saw images in my mind's eye: the lavish parties, the luxurious trips, the feeling of invincibility. But these images were quickly overshadowed by others - the missed opportunities, the impulsive decisions, the constant cheating that had ruined my relationships. It was as if my life was being in a filmplayed out and I was

48

sitting in the audience, unable to change the plot. The frustration at my own inability to extricate myself from this mental quagmire only made it worse. I would have given years of my life to undo the mistakes I made back then. With the knowledge and maturity of today, I would do things differently - more consciously, more mindfully and with more appreciation for the things that really matter. It hurts to know that you've wasted so many opportunities, damaged so many relationships through your own stupidity or selfishness. But unfortunately, there is no rewind button in life.

This thought often torments me: **What if I had acted differently back then?**

In 2009, I met my second wife - a true angel in human form. She came into my life at a time when I had almost nothing left to give. I was empty inside, burnt out, a shadow of myself.

The pressure and the shame of my failure had driven me to the brink of despair. I had already bought some pills and considered poisoning myself with car exhaust fumes. I was just waiting for the right moment. The darkness that surrounded me seemed impenetrable and I was convinced that there was no way out.

But she, this woman with the gentle eyes and unshakeable patience, managed to pull me out of this darkness. With words that didn't lecture, with gestures that said more than a thousand conversations. She held out her hand to me when I had long since given up looking for one. She managed to dispel the gloomy thoughts and helped me to slowly pick myself up again. It was as if she had seen something in me that I could no longer recognise myself.

We got married in 2010, and from then on a new phase of my life began. Slowly, step by step, I was able to build a new life for myself as a web designer and photographer. It was hard work, and there were many nights when I sat at the computer, my head full of doubts. But things were looking up, and with every new job, every successful project, a little more self-confidence returned.

Our lives developed in a great direction. The first few years were full of hope and new opportunities. But the demons of my past remained, lurking in the background and waiting for moments of weakness. My dissatisfaction and quiet sadness about what could have been would not let me go. It was as if I was fighting an inner battle that no one could see. The depression came back, deeper and more insidious than ever before. It wasn't just short moments of sadness, but long, dark phases that enveloped me like a cold fog.

I felt trapped, all I wanted to do was break out, start somewhere new - alone, without the burden of the past and without the expectations I had placed on myself. I dreamed of leaving everything behind, of starting a new project in a place that had nothing to do with my previous life.

I didn't know exactly why I felt that way. Maybe it was the hope of a new beginning, the idea that somewhere out there was a simple key to happiness. But my depression was stubborn and made every step difficult. It made me look for escape routes that were sometimes anything but healthy.

Being an Easy Rider or the attempt to realise missed dreams

It's a cliché in the book: men in midlife crisis buy a motorbike. Of course, I wasn't spared this phenomenon either. In my youth, I never had the time or the means to buy a motorbike, but the desire to do so always lay dormant in me. It was this image of freedom, the feeling of wind and speed that fascinated me - a symbol of leaving everything behind and simply riding without looking back. But life had other plans, and the dream of the bike disappeared for a long time behind obligations and everyday life.

Then came 2019: one evening, after a particularly stressful day, I was sitting on my couch and aimlessly scrolling through my feed. Suddenly, I came across an article: With a car driving licence and the addition B196, you can now also drive 125cc motorbikes. That made me sit up and take notice. Suddenly this long-suppressed dream was back, within my grasp. The decision was made quickly, like an inner impulse that I couldn't ignore. No sooner said than done: that same week, I visited an old friend who ran a driving school and signed up for the B196 course.

A weekend of theory and a few driving lessons, no exams - just the feeling of finally fulfilling a childhood dream. It was simple, uncomplicated and exactly what I needed at that moment. For 1,700 euros, I got what I forhad been longing : the right to finally sit on a motorbike. Four weeks later, I was holding my new driving licence in my hand, and with a palpitating heart that I hadn't felt for a long time, I drove off to buy my first bike - a small 125cc Suzuki. Not the big bike I once dreamed of, but enough to make me feel alive again.

The first journey home from Spandau was an experience I will never forget. The engine hummed beneath me, the roads whizzed by and the wind brushed my face. It was like travelling back in time, as if I was the 20-year-old boy who was finally fulfilling the dream he had carried around with him for so long. To be cool for once, to feel the admiring glances of passers-by, the envious looks of drivers in traffic jams - it was like a silent nod from the universe telling me: "Well done."

Riding a motorbike was more than just a hobby for me. It was a symbol of my personal freedom and a tool to see the world with new eyes.

My plan was to ride around on my motorbike with my camera and photo equipment and look for new motifs. At the time, I had discovered photography for myself and it was as if I had found a hidden treasure within me. The old creative fire that had been dormant in me since the GDR days suddenly flared up again. I began to see landscapes, people and streets with a completely different eye - not just as a backdrop, but as living scenes waiting to be captured.

There was another aspect that made this time so special: the people I was able to get to know. The motorbike community is like its own little world, full of characters and stories. I was drawn out at the weekends - to meetings, tours and little journeys of discovery.

And of course there were the women I had always admired: women with their own styles, tattooed arms, who showed that beauty has many facets. There was something untamed about these women, something that spoke to me and reminded me why I have always been fascinated by people who went their own way.

I felt an increasing desire for a new experience. It wasn't that I was missing anything at home - everything was fine sexually, I lived in a lovingly furnished home, had a great wife by my side who gave me support and love. And yet there was this inner restlessness, a whisper in the back of my mind that drove me to look for more. It wasn't even the physical desire that lured me, but rather the allure of the unknown, the excitement of being admired again and rekindling the spark of youthful adventure.

How should I describe it? My wife has often told me that she finds me attractive, that she desires and loves me. But praise from the person who has known you for years sometimes feels different, almost like a well-known refrain from an old song.

And this is where my biggest challenges began. I longed for recognition, for being adored by strange women, for the rush that comes with the hunting instinct.

It was like an old, archaic longing that awoke in me and could no longer be restrained. So what did I do? I downloaded various dating apps, installed them on my mobile phone and started chatting - first out of curiosity, then out of a mixture of excitement and euphoria.

I think I can say that I am attractive and sporty. For my 50 years, at least that's what others say, I still look "bomb". I still have all my hair, there's not a single grey one, and thanks to constant training I keep a slim figure with well-defined muscles. My clothing style tends towards military style - robust jackets, cargo trousers, cool boots. There's something militant about it and many women like it. It wasn't just a look, it was an attitude. A message that said: "I'm ready, I'm strong, I'm different."

This was also reflected in my hobbies. I was always the type who loved action-packed, exciting activities: airsoft, wakeboarding, paragliding, kiting, archery and hunting. My boot was always packed, a small arsenal of sports equipment ready for the next adrenaline rush. My mates knew that a call to me always resulted in a spontaneous, exciting idea. I was the type who couldn't tolerate boredom, who was always on the move, "Mr Action", as my friends sometimes called me.

Even as a father of four grown-up sons, I always wanted to be a role model, the "cool" dad who was up for any adventure at the weekend. The fact that I was only ever the 'weekend dad' spurred me on to make every minute together with my children something special. Berlin and Brandenburg offered the perfect playground for this - lakes, forests and an endless range of leisure activities, which I utilised to the last drop. From canoe trips to overnight stays in a tent, where we sat around the campfire together and told stories - my boys would always remember that Dad had the best ideas.

There was a new activity on the programme every fortnight. Over the years, we tried almost everything you could think of that was possible with children. I was always on the move, always looking for the next highlight. And when I was travelling without the boys, I knew exactly what effect I had on women. I had often been told that I was a handsome man with striking features and a determined look. To be honest, I never saw myself as a pretty boy. I much more wanted to be perceived as a fighter - as someone who bites through life, who keeps getting back up despite all the setbacks.

And that's exactly what I was looking for in the encounters on these dating apps: validation, the electrifying moment of flirtation, the game of looks and words that made me feel like I was still in the running, still desired and strong. Part of me knew I already had everything I needed, but another part of me, the part that had a-woken in menopause, wanted to feel the world, wanted adventure and the exhilarating feeling of being rediscovered.

So I took a few chic pictures of myself with my camera, which captured every detail perfectly. A portrait in a military-style jacket, leaning casually against my motorbike, and a picture with my beaming smile - the perfect mix of strength and charm. Uploaded, sent, and it wasn't long before the first messages from the ladies started rolling in. A tingling sensation ran down my spine as my mobile phone kept vibrating. It was like a game where I knew the rules but had to explore the playing field anew.

As my mum had brought me up to be a gentleman, I always wrote back to the ladies with respect and decency. No crude chat-up lines, no hasty questions, but genuine interest and a touch of humour.

This seemed to set me apart from the many others of my kind, at least that's what the women told me. "You're different," they wrote, "finally a man who can listen." I had to smile. How little it sometimes takes to stand out from the crowd.

Some women were particularly persistent and wanted a date straight away. But I held back, felt my way round, chatted and made phone calls at first. The thought of whether I was perhaps on the wrong track remained in the back of my mind. But I told myself that it was just words, not touching, not crossing an invisible line. "It's just writing," I told myself, "not adultery."

I switched to WhatsApp with some of the women, and things got more intense there. The messages became more personal, the emojis more flirtatious, and the game of words took on a new, exciting dynamic.

I remained a gentleman, at least at first, but apparently that was too slow for some ladies. To keep me on my toes and show me that they were genuinely interested, pictures started to trickle in - and not just any pictures, but photos that were so offensive and seductive that they made my heart beat faster . What man can resist that, especially when a woman makes you feel irresistible?

Then I got to know Isabell. Her profile immediately caught my eye. This woman radiated a mixture of adventurousness and mystery. She had long, wavy red hair that danced in the wind in her profile pictures and a smile that was both playful and challenging. It didn't take long for her to make the first move. "Well, handsome man, are you bored? What are you doing right now?" This message was original, unlike the usual, unimaginative greetings such as "Hi" or the dull "Hello".

I just happened to be at Müggelsee, one of my favourite places in Berlin. The lake was glistening in the sunlight and I had just pumped up my SUP, ready to do a few laps. A simple text seemed too boring for me. So I took my mobile phone, filmed the beach, the glistening surface of the water and sent her the video. Isabell was delighted. Her reply came promptly, a voice message in which her laughter sounded like music. "Wow, you know how to impress a woman!" she said.

Our conversation quickly picked up speed. It was as if we had known each other forever. She told me that she also rode a motorbike, a Kawasaki Z650, and I could picture her immediately: Isabell, her hair in the wind, the leather jacket with all the patches that she wore proudly. Two days later, a big biker meeting was planned in Berlin, and we decided to meet there and ride up together on our motorbikes.

The thought of driving through the streets of Berlin with her, the noise of the engine in the background and the wind in my face, made my heart beat faster. It felt like a return to something I thought I had lost - freedom, adventure, a touch of rebellion.

Isabell - or why we idiots cheat

Isabell - even the name sounded like a promise of adventure and danger. She was 1.75 metres tall, a woman who immediately attracted attention as soon as she entered a room. Her long, bright red hair fell down her back like a waterfall and her body was a canvas of tattoos, each with its own story, each a small work of art. She had large, shapely breasts and a figure that was the perfect blend of curves and fitness. But it wasn't just her looks that mesmerised me. She had that spark in her eyes, that irrepressible, wild something that made every moment with her unpredictable. She was 45, but easily looked ten years younger. Her skin was smooth and firm, without a single wrinkle, and her bum - it was simply incredible, as if it deserved its own chapter in a novel.

Isabell was a programmer, just as I worked in the digital world in the broadest sense. We immediately hit it off on this technical level, which often seemed dry to outsiders, but gave us a special bond.

No children, she told me, although she always wanted some. But the right partner who could have shared this adventure with her had never crossed her path. When I told her about my four grown-up sons and my large family, she beamed at me as if I had just shown her the most exciting book in the world. She seemed to lose herself in this idea, in a world that had always remained just a vision for her.

Her scent was unmistakable. A hint of vanilla and something floral that I couldn't name - I was instantly mesmerised by her. Her teeth were gleaming white, the smile totally natural, and her freckles scattered across a flawless face. She looked like a total work of art, created to blow the minds of men like me. And there she was, the woman who was everything I had ever wanted.

She obviously liked me just as much. She didn't take her eyes off me for a second, played with her hair and gave me a smile. My heart beat faster, my hands became moist and I was enchanted. In my head, I was already imagining what it would be like to kiss her, touch her, seduce her...

We left the motorbikes and sat down in a small café not far from the road. Her gait was elegant, almost dance-like. Everything about her radiated grace and self-confidence. The other guys at the biker meeting gave me envious looks when they saw us together. I could almost hear their thoughts: "What a lucky guy!" And I enjoyed it. I savoured every second of this admiration.

When we started talking, spoke she with an intelligence that mesmerised me. No empty words, no banal banter - she was clever, profound and had something to say. She talked about her travels, about faraway countries and cultures, about her love of art and photography. Her voice was soft and the sound of it seemed to go straight to my heart. I could have just listened for hours as she talked about her adventures with shining eyes. Her eyes kept meeting mine and it was as if the world around us slowed down.

This woman was a dangerous mixture of intelligence and sex appeal. Not only an eye-catcher on the outside, but also someone who could inspire with her sharp mind and wit. That made her doubly dangerous.

I've never had much use for superficial beauties, women who hid behind artificial appearances. But Isabell was different. She was "fully tuned", as they say - lips, hair, breasts, tattoos even on her nose - and yet she seemed completely natural in her manner. Her little freckles scattered across her nose and cheeks made her unique. They gave her something playful that I just loved.

Every fibre in me wanted to take her in my arms, kiss her, freeze the moment so that it would never end. But I remembered my mum's advice: "On a first date, just look, don't touch." And that advice was worth its weight in gold. I've always done well with this strategy. Women appreciated it - it showed decency, self-control and respect. And I knew that this was the key to creating not just fleeting moments, but real connections.

The date for a new date seemed only a matter of time. When she got on her 'stove', I followed her every move with a heartbeat that almost drove me crazy.

The sight of her perfectly shaped bum stretched out on the bench made my heart beat faster. She looked really cool on her heavy stove, which was actually far too high for her. She just managed to touch the ground with the tips of her feet.

She slowly rolled off, and I could only hope that she would turn round one last time - one last look, a sign that the date had been just as magical for her as it had been for me.

And sure enough, a few metres further on she stopped, turned to me, raised her helmet visor and sent me an air kiss. It was an electrifying moment that went right through me. I made a heart sign with my hands and she smiled before closing the visor again and driving off. The roar of her engine became quieter until it finally faded into the distance. That's when I knew that she had been just as much in love with me as I was.

The ride home on my own motorbike felt like a mixture of triumph and confusion. Her eyes, her laugh, the way she spoke - it all played on a continuous loop in my head. But as the adrenaline wore off, reason set in. I decided not to jeopardise my marriage.

I told myself that those moments with Isabell were a little gift, a hint of adventure that had shown me that I was still alive. "You've had these wonderful hours," I told myself, "and now that's enough."

But the next few days showed that it wasn't that simple. She haunted my thoughts as if she were a ghost that had taken up residence in my dreams. My mobile phone kept flashing and her name appeared on the screen. Every time I read her message, I was drawn back to that moment at the café, to the sparkle in her eyes, to her laughter. "Why are you so reserved?" she wrote. "I can't stop thinking about you. I think I have a crush on you. Let's meet again soon."

It was as if there was an invisible bond between us that I could neither ignore nor break. I finally gave in and we arranged to meet at her house.

Märkisches Viertel in Berlin, prefabricated housing, predominantly migrant neighbourhood, all pretty run-down, dirty and covered in graffiti. I just thought: My God, I hope your flat doesn't look the same.

When I rang her doorbell, I felt my heart pounding in my chest. She opened the door and looked like she had just stepped out of a glossy magazine - perfectly styled, inviting and yet with this unapproachable aura that captivated me.

Her flat was a revelation. It was not only neat and clean, but warm and inviting, as if she had planted a part of her personality in every nook and cranny. The furniture was elegant and stylish, like something out of a catalogue I like to flick through myself, and the walls were littered with photos of her travels, her family and her friends. Every picture told a story, every souvenir from exotic lands whispered of adventures and moments she had experienced. So the neighbourhood, the house and the whole environment didn't match her flat at all.

As I looked at the photos and lost myself in the stories they told, I heard the clink of ice cubes from the kitchen. She was preparing cocktails and the scent of lime and mint wafted over to me. I took a moment to breathe in deeply and soak up the atmosphere. **Everything felt right, almost too right.**

She just shouted: "Angel, why don't you sit on the balcony?" I replied: "Dream girl, I find your pictures fascinating." She replied: "You're so cute, no bloke has ever looked at them."

I couldn't stop myself from saying: "Do you have so many blokes over?" She laughed: "You doofus, come on now, I've got something tasty for you."

This lightness, this mutual teasing - it just felt good, almost like being in a small, perfect world that only belonged to the two of us for that moment.

Then she came out onto the balcony with two glasses in her hand. She sat down next to me, her proximity made me nervous and electrified me at the same time. We sat there for a moment, silent, while our eyes met and we had a whole conversation without words.

We raised our glasses to each other and I took a sip. Delicious - a fruit cocktail with a small dash of alcohol, just enough to tingle but not too heavy.

"Wow, it tastes really good," I said, looking at her. "I'm glad you like it," she replied with her radiant smile. "This is my speciality cocktail. For special guests." I grinned: "Special guests? So you're a cocktail bar for men after all?" She laughed out loud: "You're impossible. No, I meant you're special, you doofus."

The ice had long since been broken and this mixture of humour, lightness and a certain tension in the air made the moment perfect. We toasted each other again, this time with a mischievous twinkle in her eyes that immediately captivated me.

Her gaze bored deep into my eyes and before I realised it, she came closer, her lips found mine and the world around us disappeared.

The kiss was gentle and tasted delicious after the cocktail. Everything that had built up inside us over the last few days was released in that moment. It was a kiss that spoke more than just words - it was a promise, an invitation to enter the forbidden, and I was ready to block out everything else to savour this moment.

I thought to myself: "Okay, if you go any further now, you'll fall for her completely. This woman is absolute madness and pure eroticism." Isabell was an apparition that pulled the rug out from under your feet.

Her presence filled the room, a mixture of dangerous attraction and a warmth that simultaneously calmed and excited me. Her lips were full and beautifully soft and that scent - a mixture of coconut milk and Jil Sander Sun - strange and yet inexplicably beguiling.

Every moment around her was a game of fire, a balancing act between desire and self-control. She then said with a cheeky grin: "Dream man, let's go over there, I want to show you my stamp collection." I couldn't help it and burst out laughing.

"Stamp collection? Really now? That's the oldest trick in the book!" I replied with a grin.

'Shut up and come with me,' she said, pulling me firmly by the hand.

So I let myself be pulled straight into her bedroom. The room was just like the rest of the flat: tasteful, cosy and surprisingly tidy. The bed was perfectly made and it smelled of her typical mix of coconut milk and perfume.

I just thought to myself: "Okay, forget the doubts. Enjoy the show."

As she slowly began to undress, the air around us felt electrically charged. I leant against the door frame and enjoyed the show.

Her skin was flawless, covered in tattoos, mostly Viking and warrior motifs, with a huge Yggdrasil with runes on her back.

What a great body, simply flawless. Her firm, large breasts drew my gaze magically and her flawless skin seemed to glow in the soft light. She was completely shaved, and I've always been extremely fond of that.

She moved with such confidence that it took my breath away. Perfectly shaved, every detail perfectly groomed - she was like a fantasy come to life.

I couldn't help it, the little one between my legs became harder than I had ever felt before. It was as if my body had a mind of its own, completely overwhelmed by her presence. Everything about her radiated sensuality, from her seductive smile to the smooth movements with which she presented herself in front of me.

"Well, do you like what you see?" she asked with a mischievous smile as she slowly approached. "And how," I barely got out, completely enraptured by this moment that seemed like something out of a dream.

Then she took her index finger and licked it slowly and seductively before rubbing it against my trousers. With a cheeky grin, she said: "But now get out of those wet clothes."

It took me a second to realise what had just happened - and then I laughed out loud. "Hahaha, what a woman!" I thought to myself. She was just incredible, so self-confident, playful and sexy that I couldn't help but follow along completely.

"Well, dream man, why are you still standing there? Hurry up!" she added as she sat down on the edge of the bed and fixed me with this seductive gaze that almost drove me crazy.

My trousers and the rest of my clothes came off in no time at all. It went faster than I would have expected and there I was, just as God made me, with a big grin and a heart that was beating like crazy.

I went over to her and stood naked in front of her, the little one stood like a one. She just said "it's like a written invitation".

She took it in her mouth and satisfied me orally, at the same time she grabbed my bum with her other hand and pushed my little one even deeper into her mouth. My face, that was so horny. I said "stop, I don't want to come yet".

I turned her round and she knelt in front of me. With one hand on her hip and one on her back, I slowly penetrated her from behind. It was indescribable

The woman was so tight, you could tell she hadn't had any children yet. I had to pull myself together not to come straight away.

I didn't realise I was still capable of it, but with the right motivation I could do even more. We had about three hours of extensive sex that day.

I realised how I was slowly but surely falling in love with her. I wanted more and I wanted it again and again.

The loving and sensual way she treated me made everything else around me fade away. It was as if the world had stopped and it was just the two of us. Her gentle smile, the sparkle in her eyes and the way she touched me with her delicate hands triggered a wave of emotions in me that I hadn't felt for a long time. It wasn't just desire - it was the validation I was missing, the feeling of being desired and admired.

Her scent, that unique mix of Jil Sander Sun and coconut milk, was like a fragrance that burned itself deep into my memory. Even now, years later, I can almost smell it as soon as I close my eyes.

And then there was her body, this flawless, seductive body full of curves and mysterious tattoos. Every time I glanced over her skin, it told me a new story, plunging me deeper into the intoxication she was offering me. With Isabell, I didn't just feel like a man - I felt like *the* man. With her incomparable manner, she managed to remind me of the version of myself that I once was: self-confident, strong and desirable. That was good for me, more than I wanted to admit. And that made it all the more difficult to let her go.

In those moments, I wanted nothing more than to stay with her, in her world full of passion, which felt so different from the orderly everyday life that awaited me at home.

But then the thought crept in: Would I jeopardise everything I had built up? At my age, would I leave everything behind and start all over again? The thought was both tempting and terrifying at the same time.

I had already been through too many new beginnings, fought too many battles to get to where I was. The doubts ate into my consciousness and made me realise that there was no easy way out, no solution that would leave everything intact.

But then there was this inner conflict - an age-old battle between reason and desire. The little friend between my legs, who had often ruled my life more than I would have liked, spoke up as usual.

At moments like this, he always seemed to get the upper hand, making me make decisions that I would later regret. And right here, at this point, I deep down knew that I was once again on the wrong path. The path that had already brought me to the limits of myself countless times.

The bomb bursts - or why we idiots trample on what we love

It was one of those quiet, depressing Sundays when the world outside seemed peaceful and yet I found myself in a storm of guilt and doubt.

The sun shone through the half-open curtains, casting dancing patterns on the walls as we lay in her bed, exhausted and still caught up in the warmth of our moment together. We'd just finished two hours of pure, copious sex, and as her breathing calmed, I lay there, the covers pulled up to my chest, feeling an unfamiliar heaviness descend on me.

A bitter aftertaste crept up my throat. Isabell was an incredible woman - wild, clever, full of life - and in her arms I felt like a man with something to offer again.

But this illusion was fragile and I suddenly realised how futile it all was. There was no future, no common perspective, only the game of hide-and-seek and my lies, which lay around us like an invisible net. The net was tightening and I knew it was only a matter of time before it would tear.

Isabell had been asking questions for weeks. Questions that I skilfully brushed aside each time with a white lie or an excuse. "Why can't you ever be here on public holidays?" - "Why don't you ever stay overnight?"

She wasn't stupid, and I knew that her mistrust was growing. But her heart was strong enough, her love for me blind enough, to overlook my lies. She wanted to believe in us. And that made everything much worse.

She had often asked me to stay the night with her and I had a different excuse every time. "I have to get up early," "It's important that I get home, I have a project." The truth was too cruel, too ugly to say: I had a wife at home, a life I was willing to risk but not give up completely. The realisation that I had kept all this from her gnawed at me.

And so we lay there, in this strange silence that suddenly became as heavy as lead. I turned my head towards her and saw her looking at me with her big, questioning eyes. Eyes that told me that she trusted me, that she would bear any truth at that moment as long as it came from me. Tears came to my eyes, involuntarily and unexpectedly. The mask I had worn for months began to crumble.

She noticed immediately. "Angel, what's wrong?" she whispered and gently pulled me into her arms. Her lips touched my temples and she stroked my back as if to protect me from whatever was bothering me. "Please tell me," she begged, and her voice was a mixture of concern and love.

This moment was the point of no return. Either I would tell the truth and risk everything, or I would continue to lie and lose her for good when the truth came out. Isabell was not the kind of woman to settle for half-truths. I knew she was a fighter, someone who wasn't easily deceived.

"Isabell," I began, my heart racing. The words wouldn't come out of my mouth. "There's something I need to tell you." Her eyes became serious, searching my gaze for clues as to what was to follow. She: "Isabell? Are we on a first name basis now?"

The moment I uttered the words, the air in the room seemed to explode. "Dream girl, I have a confession to make, but please don't be angry..."

Her eyes, which had previously glowed with warmth and trust, narrowed to narrow slits. She sat up, the blanket slipping off her shoulders. Her voice was icy as she said, "Tell me what's going on right now, but I can guess..."

The loving look that had comforted me until then was blown away. Her face hardened and it was as if an invisible wall had gone up between us. The moment that had just connected us had vanished in a split second. My heart was pounding and my hands were shaking, as I uttered the words I could no longer take back: "Dream girl, I'm married..."

It was as if I had detonated a bomb. She jumped out of bed, her face contorted with unbridled rage and her eyes seemed to spark. "I knew it! I knew it! I knew it!" she shouted, her voice thick with anger. "Are you out of your mind?" "What kind of sick arsehole are you?" "Get out now, you piece of shit! Get out, get out, raaaaaaaaaaaaout!"

Before I knew what was happening to me, she was already naked as she was at the front door, which she tore open with a bang. Isabell stood naked in front of me, her muscles tense, her hands clenched into fists. "Get out of my flat! OUT!" she shouted. The fact was: resistance was futile.

I hastily grabbed my trousers, shirt, fanny pack and jacket, while her voice continued to sweep through the flat like a storm. "Get out!" she shouted again and again, her anger so raw and unbridled that my knees almost trembled.

I wanted to say something, stammer an apology, anything that could save the situation. But there was no room for words on her face. Her cheeks were flushed, tears were in her eyes, but she held them back - out of pride, out of anger, out of pain. The woman who had just been my whole world had turned into an enemy, and it was all my fault.

She threw my boots into the corridor one after the other with the words "There, you arsehole" and slammed the door shut. Both boots hit the door opposite like anti-aircraft shells. I often wear Haix military boots and they weigh a bit because of the steel toecaps. The impacts really rattled.

I could still quietly hear her having a crying fit behind the door. Any of the neighbours who weren't awake yet were certainly all awake now.

Stupid arsehole that I was, I had once again brought it on myself with my completely barmy behaviour.

I stood there, in the hallway of the twelve-storey prefabricated building in the Märkisches Viertel, naked with all my clothes strewn around the corridor. I could still hear Isabell's angry sobs through the closed door. My shoes were lying across the corridor.

The hallway was barren and sterile, with that unmistakable smell of cleaning products and stale air. The neon lights on the ceiling flickered slightly and I heard the roar of a hoover somewhere in the distance. The silence after the storm was almost deafening.

Suddenly the door, which had just been hit by my boots, opened and the neighbour from opposite stepped out. Blonde, about 35 years old and very attractive. The look on her face was a mixture of astonishment and question marks. Her eyes widened when she saw me - half naked, dressed only in my pants and the rest of my clothes in my   hand.

"Well, Sunday didn't go as planned, did it?" Her tone was sarcastic.

I looked at her and a laugh escaped me. In view of the whole bizarre scene, I could no longer control myself. "Nah, nah, everything's great, I'll be fine", while I finally put on my pants. In truth, I didn't realise anything. I thought I was on a film shoot, the whole situation was so bizarre.

The neighbour just shook her head, mumbled something like, "Only crazy people and idiots here" and closed her door with an energetic bang.

Before I could organise my thoughts, another door opened. The one to the right of Isabell's flat. The neighbour, a tall, southern-looking man with dark curls and a strange look, stepped out.

He was wearing a simple T-shirt over a big beer belly and a pair of almost white pants with an opening. Like in the Werner Beinhart film, the caretaker guy in the scene with the key to the boiler room.

"Brother, what are you doing? Are you all right? Doing loud here, you say?" His eyes looked at me sceptically and I could see him trying to grasp the situation.

"Yes, yes, everything's fine," I replied as I tried to put my shoes on, leaning against the wall so as not to lose my balance.

The guy's broken German and the picture of the pants with the opening did the rest for me. I couldn't contain myself and was almost on the floor laughing. I already had tears in my eyes. It was really cinematic and one of the coolest things I've ever experienced in my life

Luckily, I had grabbed my fanny pack with the car keys in all the hustle and bustle. If I'd lost that too, the day would have turned into a complete fiasco - and that would have been the just punishment for all the nonsense I'd got up to.

I didn't wait for the lift, but walked down the seven floors to the exit. The silence in the car felt strange, like a gentle echo after a loud bang. I just thought: My God, what a crazy move. I stayed in the car for a while to calm down a bit. I looked up at Isabell's flat. I could see the bedroom window from the car, hoping she might be looking down. I then picked up my mobile phone and wrote her a message. But instead of two blue ticks, there was only one. She had obviously already blocked me, as her profile picture was no longer visible. What a bummer. I had just lost my dream woman, I thought.

I started the engine and drove aimlessly through the streets, the familiar houses and trees passing me by like a blurred film strip.

After a while, when my thoughts calmed down a bit, I decided to stop off at a small café to calm down a little.

The sweet smell of fresh pastries and coffee greeted me and I sat down at a table in the corner. I ordered a cup of tea and a croissant, sank into the chair and felt the tension slowly ease. But as I sat there, the memories of the last few hours flooded back and before I could stop myself, I began to grin quietly to myself. Because despite the sadness of losing this great woman, the whole thing was so horny and strange that I could only laugh about it. The guy with the beer belly and the chick from across the street - hahaha, how cool. How they looked!

It was the kind of laugh you only have when you fully realise the absurdity of the moment. A laugh that can't be stopped, even when you know it's out of place. I had to pull myself together not to burst out laughing while covering my face with my hand.

The other guests gave me furtive glances and I could imagine what they were thinking: "This guy isn't all there. Maybe he's on drugs or has a few too many revolutions in his head." But I didn't care. I kept laughing, tears in eyes myand had to force myself to calm down.

Now that I'm sitting here writing these lines, the laughter is coming back. Yes, it was a crazy, film-like action - a scene you never forget. Even when I see my life pass me by at the time of my death, it will be one of those moments that I will remember and that will bring a final, ironic smile to my face.

Of course, there was radio silence with Isabell after this episode. She had blocked me on all channels and I knew I deserved it. It felt like I had cut a wire that had held an important connection. In the silence after the catastrophe, all that remained was the echo of my decisions and the knowledge that some moments, however bizarre, are the lessons that shape us the most.

Over the next few days and weeks, I felt an unbearable heartache that hit me harder than I could ever have imagined. I missed Isabell in a way that literally tore me apart. Every moment without her was agony and I only now realised that it wasn't just the thrill or the physical attraction - it was more. Much more. There was a connection, a deep longing that I had never found in my everyday life. But as much as I sank into my grief, I also felt a strange kind of liberation. The affair was over, the eternal game of hide-and-seek and the fear that Isabell might turn up at my house in revenge and blow the whistle were gone.

But as fate sometimes plays out, my relief was short-lived. One evening, it was already late and I was lying on the couch when my mobile phone suddenly vibrated. A familiar "pling" and the screen lit up: a WhatsApp message from Isabell. My heart skipped a beat. I stared at the display as if I'd seen a ghost.

The message was short, but it made my heart race: "Angel, I love you so much. Please let's talk and come back to me." I read the words over and over again, unable to realise that they really came from her. Part of me wanted to jump up and go to her immediately, wanted to undo the past weeks and rekindle all the feelings that had been between us. And yes, I admit it - I felt overjoyed. This was the selfish me, the part of me that believed I could have it all without fear of consequences.

Isabelle's apology rang in my head like a sweet promise. She wanted me back, despite everything. "I have her now," I thought. A thought so selfish that it gave me a stab myself. I imagined how I could continue my double life: Isabell as my lover, my wife at home, a game that I controlled according to my rules. The thought of it filled me with a dark satisfaction.

"Maybe she finally got it," I muttered to myself as I moved my fingers shakily across the display to answer. My mind knew what I was doing was wrong. But my heart - or maybe it was just my desire for validation and passion - was crying out for more. Isabell was like an addiction to me, and like any addict, I told myself that I had everything under control. That I would manage to unite both worlds without one of them collapsing.

But deep down, I knew it wasn't that simple. Isabell wasn't the kind of woman who would settle for the role of mistress. And I wasn't the kind of man who stuck to the easy solutions. It was only a matter of time before the house of cards I had so carefully built would start to totter again.

The affair dragged on for the next year and we found ourselves in a routine that felt exciting and dangerous at the same time. We met every 5 to 14 days, but it was no longer just secret rendezvous for physical closeness. We began to extend our lives together as if we were a real couple, spending time on the little adventures of everyday life. We went on long rides on our motorbikes, the wind whipping in our faces and giving us a sense of freedom that only existed in this form when we were together. It was as if the world belonged to just the two of us for those hours.

Sport was another link. We lifted weights together, spurred each other on and laughed about the little competitions we had. Our dynamic was explosive, full of tension and an underlying sizzle that could turn into passion at any time. After these sweat-inducing training sessions, many evenings ended in their flat, where showering together was almost a ritual. The hot steam, the feeling of water running over our heated bodies and the sex in the shower. The sports dates always ended with us going down on each other and having mega hot sex. I loved giving her oral sex and the way she screamed and came after just a few moments was just incredible. I always had to pinch her to get her to keep the volume down - after all, I didn't want us to get a visit from the police.

It wasn't just the adventure or the forbidden nature of our meetings, but the way she laughed, the way she looked at me like I was the only man she ever wanted. She had an indescribable energy, a presence that filled every room she entered. Her voice was full of vibrancy and her smile radiated a warmth that was addictive.

The things we did together made it almost impossible to ignore reality. The cinema, the exhibitions, the conversations felt like a marriage. Some days I wondered how long I could keep up the game without everything collapsing like a house of cards. But these thoughts quickly faded when we were together and reason was drowned out by the urgency of the moment.

One example: After sport, we showered together at her place, she was into sex if the neighbours noticed. She pulled me out of the shower and onto her balcony. We were both naked and still completely wet from the shower. My little one was standing like a rock because I was completely horny for her and her big, firm breasts were swaying back and forth. The tattoos on her back were like stories you could look at when you took her from behind. The way she walked, the way she smelled, the way she looked, her great bum, I was infatuated with her every time.

She pushed me onto the garden bench on her balcony and pleasured me orally. Just before I came, she sat on me and moaned with pleasure as I poured myself into her.

This went on for a few hours, she couldn't get enough of sex with me. I constantly had to cover her mouth so that the neighbours didn't call the police. But she kept squealing loudly anyway. I enjoyed it, that great body and her big breasts that bobbed up and down, a dream. I hoped there would never be an end to it.

It actually felt like a real relationship, one that was full of intensity and passion and where there were no half measures. That day, after we had lost ourselves in a storm of feelings and desire, she stood barefoot in the kitchen, cooking our meal and smiling at me from time to time as if I were the centre of her world. The smell of freshly roasted herbs and garlic filled the small flat and gave the moment an almost cosy warmth that settled deep inside me. It was a moment that felt real - so real that it hurt.

After we had eaten, she disappeared briefly into the next room and returned with a letter in her hand. Her eyes were soft and her gaze held a hint of nervousness.

She handed me the letter and said in a low voice: "Baby, you are the man of my dreams, I love you so unspeakably. Please read this letter in peace, because it says what I feel and feel for you." Her words echoed in my head as I took the letter. The note felt heavier than it was - full of unspoken thoughts and feelings.

On the way home, I pulled into a side street, switched off the engine and opened the letter. With shaky hands and a sinking feeling in my stomach, I began to read. She had put her feelings into every word. She recalled all the little and big moments we had shared - the trips on our motorbikes, the dates full of laughter, the secret glances in crowded rooms that revealed how we felt about each other. She wrote how much she had suffered from our break-up and that the pain was still deep inside her. Every sentence was an echo of what I felt deep inside myself but never wanted to admit.

She talked about how perfect we were for each other, how we com-plemented each other and how she firmly believed that she was the one for me. Her words were a mixture of longing and urgency. She described our sensual, almost limitless sex, this physical connection that was so intense that she said she had never experienced such passion before.

She begged me to finally make a decision, to separate and start a new life with her. The idea of starting over together somewhere else suddenly no longer sounded like an illusion, but like a real possibility.

At the end of the letter, she asked me to marry her. She wrote: "Please think about what it would be like to wake up next to me every morning, to travel the world with me and to live a life that belongs only to us." Her words pierced me, creating a chasm in my chest that felt like an endless void. I suddenly realised how much I had hurt her and the emotional spiral I had dragged her into.

I sat in the car like a child, holding the letter with both hands and unable to hold back the tears. The tears ran down my face and I could feel the salty taste on my lips. I cried uncontrollably because I knew I was too much of a coward to make a fresh start with this amazing woman. I didn't feel like going through another divorce and all the struggle that would entail. I just didn't have the strength to fight anymore. I realise now as I write that all those last sentences started with "I" - what a fucking egotist I am.

It was a moment of remorse, self-realisation and overwhelming pain. I had hurt her so many times, she who had given me everything she had. And I knew that it was my own fault that I had put us both in this untenable situation. It was a long time before I got a grip on myself again, put my hands around the steering wheel and took a deep breath.

I then didn't see Isabell for a fortnight. I had contracted coronavirus and didn't want to put her at risk.

The Judgement Day - Karma strikes

Sometimes, when you look back, you realise that life is a bit like a boomerang: everything you send out comes back to you at some point. And that's how it was for me. All the decisions I had made -

75

the good ones, the bad ones and, above all, the selfish ones - had built up over the years like a ticking time bomb.

It came as it had to. I, the complete idiot, had hidden Isabell's love letter in an old jacket. Why? Because it was the most beautiful, the most sincere love letter I had ever received in my life. I couldn't bring myself to throw it away. It was a piece of memory that reminded me how much I had been desired and loved, how alive I had felt. A stupid, sentimental mistake that was to be my undoing.

One day, completely out of the blue, my wife decided to start the spring clean with a thorough wash of my old cloth jackets. The jakkets that I hadn't worn for a long time were also to be cleaned. I, the complete idiot, had long forgotten about the letter. Instead of destroying it immediately after reading it or hiding it in a safer place, it was still in my inside pocket, a ticking paper time bomb.

The classic, as they say. We men are sometimes incredibly naive - the old hunter behaviour that is in us, the collecting and hoarding of trophies, even if they could destroy our lives.

And then the inevitable happened. The moment that would change everything. **The shitty letter - she found it**

The super-GAU. The air in the flat seemed to condense abruptly when I heard her voice from the living room, a choked, trembling "What is this?" Her tone left no doubt: she had discovered it.

The day had already got off to a bad start anyway, with a letter from the tax office a hefty tax . announcing But according to demandOkham's law, that was just the beginning. It got worse. Much worse.

I had no choice, no hiding place, no place to retreat to. I had to confess everything - every single painful truth, deep into the night. The words came hesitantly, as if I had to tear each piece of my guilt out of me one by one.

My wife sat in front of me, her eyes reddened, tears streaming down her cheeks in a never-ending flood. She had a veritable crying fit.

Her hands were shaking and her whole appearance was a mixture of pain, confusion and pure, naked disappointment. It was as if I had shattered the core of her world and she was now standing in front of the shards, unable to understand how it could have come to this.

At that moment, I realised how much she had loved me all those years, how deep her feelings really were. I had always thought that love was a natural give and take, a silent contract that you forget to appreciate over time. But now I saw that everything she did was out of that love - the home she created for us, the warmth she wove around us, the care in every detail of our lives.

And I, the complete idiot, had taken it all for granted. I had never really looked, never understood that it was she who held the foundation of our lives while I, in my selfishness and stupidity, sought another way. The realisation came too late and the regret felt like a sword that was eating me from the inside out. I wanted to turn back time, I wanted to undo all the unsaid and all the hurt. But now I was just a man who had realised too late what he had - and what he might lose forever.

It hurt to realise how blind I had been. I, the stupid one, had not recognised all that she had done for us and had instead perceived it as constriction and clinging. Now, in this moment, I felt a deep sadness that completely paralysed me. I couldn't cope at all, the feelings of guilt and remorse gnawed at me like hungry animals. At the same time, however, it also felt like a liberating blow. This whole messy situation had worn me down.

I had wanted to end the affair with Isabell for a long time, but it always seemed impossible to break away. The attraction was too strong, the web of lies that I had woven around myself was too complicated. And there was always this nagging fear that she would turn up at our house out of anger if I broke it off.

Never underestimate the wisdom of a woman

And Isabell was clever. She had found out more about me than I could ever have imagined. It was during one of our outings together that us.one of my customers ran into He addressed me by my full name and mentioned the name of my company several times. Up until that point, Isabell had only known me by my first name and had never asked what my real name was. But this chance moment was enough to arouse her curiosity.

She went home, sat down at her computer and started researching. She was not only beautiful and seductive, but also clever and persistent.

An extract from the commercial register was all she needed to find out not only my business connections but also my home address. I only found out much later that she had visited my address and taken a photo of the doorbell sign - proof that hung over me like a sword of Damocles.

That was after our first separation, after I had confessed to her that I was married. It was her way of showing me that she knew everything and that she wasn't afraid to use this information.

At one of our last meetings, she held the photo in front of my nose. Her eyes flashed in a way that sent a cold shiver down my spine.

"Baby," she said with a smile that was more like a threat, "don't ever make me mad. You know what vendetta means."

The words echoed in my head. I knew that a separation from her would be anything but smooth. The prospect of her turning up at my house and my wife everythingtelling was more than real. The fear of this kept me trapped, kept me going in this toxic spiral. It was a game in which I had all the cards against me and the realisation came too late.

The super-GAU day changed everything. I was sitting in the living room, my wife opposite me, her eyes red and swollen from crying. The air was heavy, full of unspoken words and the tension that comes with the end of an era. I clutched my mobile phone tightly as if it was the last thing that connected me to Isabell.

My wife demanded in a firm voice that I call Isabell and end the affair - now, immediately, in front of her. The room seemed to be spinning and I felt hot and cold at the same time.

With trembling fingers, I dialled the number I knew by heart and pressed "Call". It only took a few seconds for her to pick up, her voice so familiar and yet so strange at that moment.

"Baby, is that you? What's wrong?" I heard her say, the hope in her voice impossible to ignore. I gathered all my courage and said: "Isabell, it's over. We can't do this anymore. I'm sorry."

Silence. Then a cry that went through me: "No, baby, please don't! Stay with me!" Her words hit me like a blow, but I held on. I hung up without saying another word and blocked her number. My heart was pounding wildly and I felt relieved and shattered at the same time. I had done it - the break had been made, but at what cost?

My wife watched me the whole time, her eyes full of pain, but also a quiet hope. Perhaps she believed that this phone call was a start, an attempt to pull us out of the shambles. The fact that she was prepared to give me a chance at all spoke volumes about her love and her will to save us. Anyone else would have thrown me out the door long ago.

The following weeks were characterised by deep grief and endless conversations. We talked long into the night about things that had long remained unspoken, about the injuries I had caused and about the insecurities that now accompanied us. It was as if we had to rebuild our relationship brick by brick. I had to confess every single moment with Isabell and explain why and why I couldn't get away from this woman.

But that didn't come without conditions. I had to change from the ground up, and that meant reprioritising my life.

My wife and our family became the centre of my life again and I was determined never to take her for granted again. She wanted to know where I was and what I was doing from then on, and I had no problem with that. I sent her my location, phoned when I was out and about and always kept her in the loop. This was not a burden for me - it was a sign of my remorse and my desire to give her back the trust I had so carelessly destroyed.

What initially seemed like a control measure became a new bond between us. We were closer than ever before, almost like in the early years of our marriage, when everything was new and exciting. Small gestures became part of our everyday life. I surprised her with small gifts, a bunch of flowers or a card with just a simple sentence: "I love you." And every time she smiled, I felt a part of my broken heart heal.

New rituals emerged that brought us even closer together. On Fridays after work, we would jump into the bathtub together, a glass of wine in our hands, while we talked and laughed. Once a month, we went to the sauna together to just relax and leave the world outside. These moments together became an anchor in our relationship, something we both looked forward to and reminded us why we were together.

These little time-outs became sacred to me. They were proof that you can find your way back to each other even after all these years and despite all your mistakes.

I had almost put everything on the line, but now I knew that love was worth fighting for. There is life after menopause, and sometimes it brings with it a new kind of love - one that is more mature, more enduring and more honest. A love that can weather the darkest storm and grow stronger in the process.

I've been a completely different man since the end of my affair with Isabell. My life has been reorganised and there are now only three priorities for me: Family, work and hobbies - and in that order. I used to be the centre of my own universe and everything revolved around my self-fulfilment and the pursuit of the next thrill. It's no wonder that back then I constantly felt like I couldn't reconcile anything.

My marriage, my self-employment, my children, my extended family, my hobbies - and then a lover. I was rushing from one aspect of my life to the next without really getting anywhere. The result was a constant state of dissatisfaction, an incessant race against the clock that eventually brought me to the edge of the abyss.

Looking back, I realise how much I torpedoed my own life and turned it into a mess. Instead of living a calm, fulfilling life, I let my desires and insatiable search for validation guide me. I allowed my "little friend" between my legs to dictate my actions and paid a high price for it.

Guys, if you recognise yourself in my story, please don't make the same mistake. Stop before the bomb explodes and everything you hold dear blows up. Cheating may seem like an exciting at timesadventure , an escape from the daily grind, but in the end it leads to nothing but wreckage and regret.

Because what are you left with in the end when everything falls apart? Divorce, stress, the life of a lonely man who hops from one affair to the next? How long do you think this lifestyle will fulfil you? With every year that passes, the energy dwindles and the chances of a new, fulfilling love grow slimmer.

We are all getting older, and that means that potential partners also have their own established lives. Women over 50 have their own routines, their own plans and often have little desire to turn their lives upside down for someone who thinks they've just discovered their second youth.

And yes, I know, the temptation of a younger woman is enticing - the youthful energy, the attractive body, the thought of hot, carefree nights. But think one step further: a younger partner often also means a desire to have children or existing toddlers or teenagers who are still in the middle of school. Do you really want to take on the challenges of nappies, school projects and teenage drama again when you're over 50? Will you have the energy when you get home after a long day at work?

I have changed because I have realised that true happiness does not lie in constant escapes and adventures, but in appreciating what I already have. My wife, my family, the little moments we spend together - these are the things that count when the noise of everyday life dies down and you find peace. And I can tell you: it's a peace that I never knew before, but that I appreciate all the more now.

For me, starting again from scratch was not an option - not after everything I had already been through. Four failed relationships, four attempts to build a new life, four bitter aftertastes of disappointment. If I had to try again, it would only have been with a woman who had no children, who was independent and financially self-sufficient, lived in her own flat and - most importantly - had no pets. I have nothing against animals, but a private zoo was the last thing I wanted to do to myself.

Looking back, I realise what an incredible asshole I was before the super-GAU.

The low point? The moment when I left my wife alone at home with a fever of 40 degrees and a coronavirus infection to drive to Isabell.

Yes, you heard right - while she lay in bed, sweating and weak, I raced off to my affair. When I think back on it today, I could kick myself in the arse. What selfish, self-absorbed behaviour. I plundered and gutted my karma account during that time until there was nothing left. And believe me, fate forgets nothing and takes its revenge sooner or later.

In my case, I was lucky in misfortune. I was given a second chance, and I seized this opportunity to lead a calmer, more honest life. But that didn't mean that the past simply disappeared. Isabell didn't let go that easily. A few weeks after our final separation, the doorbell rang and a nondescript parcel addressed to my wife was delivered.

I didn't suspect anything good, and my premonition came true when my wife opened the parcel. Inside was a cynical letter of abuse in which Isabell described in detail what an a...ch I was. She had included all the gifts I had ever given her - jewellery, perfume and small, meaningful things that would have been romantic in other contexts.

But here they became sharp blades that pierced my heart. The letter also said that I wanted to propose to her and was planning to move in with her. The content was like a perfidious stab aimed at destroying the last hope my wife might still have had.

But my wife? She surprised me once again. She took the parcel and the letter, looked at me - not with reproach, but with a mixture of determination and a touch of pity. She went to the door, descended the stairs, and I followed her with a pounding heart. At the bottom of the bin, she paused and gave me a look that said, "This is the end of the line." With a loud laugh, she threw the parcel into the bin, slammed the lid shut and let it snap shut with a loud bang.

What a strong woman. At that moment, I realised that she wasn't just my partner - she was the pillar that supported our life together, who gave me a third chance where others would have left long ago. I couldn't help but feel respect and love for this woman who, despite everything, was willing to rebuild our lives.

Let's put it this way - I deserved to be punched in the face. All because I was such a wimp and couldn't cope with my environment. Time and time again, I fell back into the same bad behaviour patterns from the past. Like a demon that had taken possession of me, I kept choosing destruction and the worst way. Conflict resolution has never been my strong point.

Instead of talking to my wife, I chose the easiest route. Looking back, it wasn't worth all the stress, but I only realise that now with a certain distance.

I haven't seen or heard from Isabell since then. Every now and then I met her in my dreams. The dreams seemed very real, and after waking up they usually kept me busy all day. I think it will take me a while to process the affair and the abrupt end and put it behind me. The whole affair was too intense and crazy for me to forget from one day to the next.

What I often ask myself is: what will it be like if we meet again by chance one day? The idea is somehow surreal, almost like a film scene in which the past and the present collide. The likelihood of this is slim, after all, we live at opposite ends of the city, separated by kilometres and the lives we have built since then. But sometimes fate plays its own games, and who knows what else it has in store for us?

When I think of this possibility, the chorus of "Don't You" by Simple Minds immediately pops into my head: Don't you, forget about me, As you walk on by, Will you call my name? When you walk

"Are you going to call my name when you walk past? Or will you just keep walking?" This thought hurts. Would she look at me? Would she smile wistfully or simply avert her gaze and walk on as if I were just a stranger from a bygone era? Or would she speak to me?

The affair with Isabell is more than just a memory - it is a chapter that is deeply etched in my memory, with all its highs and lows, its intoxicating passion and the bitter consequences I paid for it.

I know that these memories will be among those that pass me by at the end of my life, when the light of life slowly goes out. A fleeting film of moments, laughter and moments of regret.

Why do we men do this to ourselves? Why do we risk everything for the fleeting thrill, for the feeling of being desired again, like in our prime? It is this insatiable search for confirmation, for the tingling sensation that pushes everyday life into the background. The urge to feel the fire that reminds us that we are still alive.

Cheating is not just an act of deceit, it is a reflection of the insecurities and fears that gnaw deep within us. The fear of ageing, the fear of no longer being enough, the fear of losing the adventure and magic of life.

But what remains afterwards? A destroyed trust, a pile of broken pieces and the realisation that the flame that burned so brightly went out too quickly and burnt everything around it. And yet, despite everything, there is a part of me that cannot simply erase the chapter with Isabell. It is a part of my history, a reminder and a faint echo that reminds me of the decisions that have made me the man I am today. A man who is looking for peace between the past and what lies ahead.

I have tried to explain why I ended up cheating so often in the last few chapters. It was a mixture of curiosity, insecurity and the urge for validation. But the phenomenon of cheating is much bigger than my own story. It affects many people, both men and women, and has many facets. But why do we do it? What drives us to take the risk of jeopardising our relationships, just for a fleeting moment of lust or adventure?

There are numerous theories that try to explain cheating, but they all ultimately lead us to a basic need: the desire for a "thrill". This kick is the thrill, the adrenaline that makes us feel that we are still alive, that we are desirable, that there is more out there than what we already have. It's often not just about sex. Cheating is often an escape from everyday life, a rebellion against routine and the feeling of being trapped.

The causes of cheating: an analysis

Based on current surveys and studies, the following can be said about male cheating in Germany:

The figures indicate a slight increase in male infidelity in recent years. In 2018, 23% of men stated that they had cheated at least once, whereas in 2020 the figure was 27%.

Cheating is not only a physical act, but also a psychological pheno-menon. It often begins in the mind of the person concerned and is the result of an inner conflict. One of the main causes is the loss of tension and excitement in the best relationship. Many people in long-term relationships feel trapped in a rut of repetition and obligations. Everyday life has replaced the passionate moments that once cha-racterised the relationship. The unexpected, the new, the adventure is missing - and that's exactly what people are looking for in an affair.

Another important factor is the desire for affirmation. Doubts arise, especially in the phase of life that is often referred to as the "male menopause". You wonder whether you are still attractive, desirable and alive. The attention of another person can intensify this feeling and lead to a real ego boost. It is an opportunity to prove to yourself that you are still capable of conquering and seducing.

But there are also deeper, emotional causes. An unfulfilled emotio-nal connection in the main relationship is often behind cheating. The feeling of not really being understood or appreciated can drive people to look elsewhere for what they are missing. It is an attempt to fill the inner vacuum created by emotional distance or misunder-standings. Here, cheating becomes compensation for the lack of in-timacy or emotional closeness.

Another often underestimated reason is the desire for variety. People are curious by nature and are looking for new experiences. An affair offers the opportunity to immerse yourself in a new world where everything is exciting and fresh. This change can be ex-hilarating, especially when everyday life is dominated by routine.

Finally, social pressure also plays a role. In a world where success is often defined by achievement, conquest and adventure, cheating can be seen as a kind of status symbol. The allure of running a se-cret parallel world can be a form of self-empowerment for some people - proof that they are still in control of their lives and write their own rules.

In many cases, cheating is less a conscious decision and more a gradual process. It starts with a harmless flirtation, a compliment, prolonged eye contact. And before you know it, you're drawn into something that has spiralled out of control. The thrill you were looking for at the beginning quickly becomes a trap in which you become entangled.

The male hunting instinct - instinct or excuse?

Another phenomenon that is often used as an explanation for cheating is the so-called male hunting instinct. This term comes up again and again when it comes to interpreting the behaviour of men in relation to their sexuality. But what does this hunting instinct really mean? Is it an innate instinct that is deeply rooted in our evolutionary history or just a convenient excuse to justify unfaithful behaviour?

The male hunting instinct is often presented as a kind of biological imperative. In this view, male behaviour is determined by an evolutionary urge to spread his genes as widely as possible. According to this theory, men are "programmed" to constantly look for new sexual opportunities. In the early history of mankind, this behaviour ensured the survival and spread of their own genes - a time when reproduction played a central role in the struggle for survival.

This drive for conquest and diversity is therefore nothing new. Humans, especially men, have always endeavoured to extend their reach - be it by building up tribal structures, fighting for territory or by tying themselves to several women. A man's success was often measured by how many partners he had, and this "spirit of conquest" has continued to a certain extent right up to the present day. Even though we no longer live in caves, these instincts remain deeply rooted in us.

But what does this mean for today? Are we still living by these Stone Age rules, or have we as modern humans developed the ability to control our urges? Many men still feel the need to 'chase' - not necessarily because they want to pass on their genes, but because the conquest itself gives a sense of power, control and validation. It is the thrill of the chase, the game of seduction and devotion that drives men. The search for the next "adventure" or the next "conquest" conveys the feeling of being alive and desirable.

In long-term relationships, however, this hunting feeling can often diminish. The relationship develops into something familiar and stable, but also predictable. At this moment, the hunting instinct is awakened again - because the adventure and the unknown that was once so exciting is now missing. In this context, cheating can be a kind of "escape" from routine, a way to experience the feeling of conquering something new and exciting again.

However, there is also the view that this hunting instinct is a convenient excuse to justify selfish behaviour. Many psychologists argue that cheating often has less to do with a biological instinct and more to do with emotional and psychological deficits. It's often about validation, the feeling of still being desired and the need for recognition - all aspects that can fall short in a stable but sometimes monotonous relationship.

Nevertheless, it is important not to regard the hunting instinct as just an "excuse". In many cases, it reflects a deep need to constantly redefine oneself. Men who feel that they are at an impasse in their lives, be it professionally or privately, often find the hunt for new sexual conquests a way to rediscover their identity. So it's not just about the physical act of cheating, but about a deeper, psychological need for self-affirmation and vitality.

This hunting instinct is therefore a double-edged sword. On the one hand, there is the evolutionary imperative that drives us to always look for new opportunities. On the other hand, it is often a symptom of deeper emotional needs that remain unfulfilled in the relationship. Whether the hunting instinct is seen as an excuse or a real drive ultimately depends on how we see ourselves and our relationships.

Cheating - but the right way? Common mistakes and why affairs blow up

When it comes to cheating, many people think they can go unnoticed and keep everything under control. But reality shows otherwise. Affairs often come to light - and not infrequently because of trivial mistakes that happen in the heat of the moment or through carelessness. The idea that you are smarter than everyone else and can keep the affair secret often proves to be deceptive. But why do so many affairs come to light? And what common mistakes lead to the affair being exposed?

1. emotional attachment to the affair

One of the most common mistakes when cheating is that it doesn't remain purely physical. An emotional bond often develops with the affair, which becomes more and more intense over time. What began as a harmless flirtation or purely sexual encounter turns into an emotional dependency. This emotional attachment leads many people to become careless. They begin to text more frequently, make secret phone calls or lose themselves in moments when their partner is unaware. The stronger the emotional connection becomes, the harder it is to act rationally - and the greater the risk of being discovered. That's exactly what you experienced with me and Isabell.

2. careless digital traces

Another typical mistake when cheating is leaving digital traces behind. In our modern world, we have countless communication channels - from text messages to WhatsApp, social media and emails. Many people underestimate how easy it is to get caught using these channels. Messages are accidentally not deleted, notifications pop up on the mobile phone display or GPS locations in apps suddenly reveal where you have actually been. Often all it takes is a small misstep, such as an inattentive moment when a suspicious message from the wrong sender pops up, to blow the whistle.

Shared devices such as computers or tablets also become a trap. All a partner has to do is browse through your browser history or access a social media platform that you have stayed logged into - and the affair is discovered.

3. changes in behaviour

A major mistake made by many people who cheat is the change in their behaviour towards their partner. Sometimes the attempt to cover up feelings of guilt becomes particularly obvious. Suddenly there is excessive attention, expensive gifts or unusual displays of affection. This may seem like a "positive" change at first, but it often looks suspicious to your partner. The sudden change can raise questions and fuel doubts. On the other hand, people who cheat often become more emotionally distant, inattentive and withdrawn. They spend more time alone, justify unexpected absences or show a growing lack of interest in the relationship. These changes are also often noticed by your partner and lead to mistrust. Guys, you're changing and you don't even realise it because it's a gradual process - if only because your affair is constantly dominating your thoughts and the desire for more sex is driving you.

4. too often the same excuses

Constant excuses are another major problem when cheating. In the beginning, spontaneous "business trips", "overtime" or "meeting friends" may still work. But the more often these excuses are used, the less credible they seem. Partners are often watchful observers, and if the stories are repeated or don't fit together, suspicion grows. Even small inconsistencies, such as different times or a lack of plausible explanations, can lead to your cover being blown.

A common mistake in this phase is to underestimate your partner's intelligence. Many people who cheat believe they can easily keep up their lies, but in reality, things rarely go undetected, especially if the stories don't fit together seamlessly.

5. underestimating the environment

One of the biggest stumbling blocks to cheating is the social environment. People forget how small the world can be and how easily information about friends, acquaintances or colleagues can leak out. A mutual friend could happen to be sitting in the same restaurant, a colleague could see the other partner's car in an unexpected place - and the first rumours are already circulating. People who cheat often underestimate the attention and memory of those around them. Even if the partner doesn't suspect anything, those around them may notice things that set the ball rolling.

In addition, affairs often occur in a professional environment or among friends, where it is even more difficult to keep everything secret. The other person in the affair can also become a risk - especially if they are emotionally involved and start to exert pressure or even threaten to disclose the affair if their needs are not met. You will learn more about this topic in another chapter. Don't get caught by anyone other than your best mate.

6. underestimating one's own reactions

After all, many people underestimate their own reactions to cheating. Whilst you may initially believe that you have everything under control, strong emotional reactions often break through over time. Feelings such as jealousy, guilt or fear of discovery can lead to people acting irrationally. These inner conflicts are difficult to hide and lead to the partner noticing changes that in turn arouse suspicion.

Cheating - You'll get caught at some point - I promise

Cheating is a risky game, and the risk of getting caught is ever-present. However, when venturing into this dangerous territory, there are some basic rules and tips that can help minimise the chances of an affair coming to light. Here are some tried and tested strategies I've developed over time - not as a free pass, but as a cautious guide to minimise the likelihood of discovery.

1. use clear names on dating portals

When you sign up on dating platforms, it is essential to never reveal your real name. It may be tempting to simply use your real name, but this opens the door to discovery. Instead, use a fantasy name that has no connection to your real identity. This will protect you from prying eyes and potential investigations by your partner.

2. affairs reveal personal details about job and family

It's tempting to make an emotional connection, but cheating should remain as impersonal as possible. Avoid telling your affair too many details about your life, your job or your family. Any hint you give could be used against you in a moment of curiosity or suspicion. Make sure that your affair only knows what is absolutely necessary. your real nameUnder no circumstances should you reveal - a false identity not only offers protection, but also makes the affair easier to control.

3. take friends on dates

A common mistake is to let friends in on the secrets of the affair. As much as you trust your friends to be loyal, the reality is that people will talk - sometimes unintentionally, sometimes because they feel morally obligated. Keep your affair top secret and avoid introducing your affair to your circle of friends or planning activities with them. The fewer people know about it, the safer you are.

4. second secret mobile phone with a separate number

A second mobile phone is essential if you are going to cheat in the long term. It should have a phone number that nobody in your private circle knows - neither friends, nor family, nor your partner. Use this mobile phone exclusively for communicating with your affair and always keep it well hidden. Avoid using your main device for the affair so as not to have risky messages or calls on an easily accessible device.

5. an invented story about career, life and family

Another effective protection is to create a fictitious life story for your affair. Make up a profession, a place of residence and a family situation that has nothing to do with your real life. This will minimise the risk of your affair coming across real details of your life or making enquiries. It is important that you remain consistent: Always stick to the same story to avoid any inconsistencies.

6. note down what you have told

It may seem excessive, but it's extremely helpful to make a note somewhere of what you've told your affair about your made-up life. Small details such as your supposed job, where you live or your family situation can easily be forgotten, especially if the affair has been going on for a long time. By keeping a discreet record, you ensure that you don't fall into the trap of making contradictory statements that could appear suspicious.

7. do not send nude pictures

One of the biggest mistakes people make in affairs is sending naked pictures. Not only can these fall into the wrong hands, but they often become leverage if the affair gets out of hand. Avoid sending compromising photos of yourself that could serve as proof of your infidelity. You never know where these pictures will end up or who might see them at some point.

8. send images only temporarily and with a time limit

If you do decide to send pictures, make sure that they are only visible temporarily. Many messenger apps such as WhatsApp offer the option to set a time limit on pictures so that they disappear automatically after a certain period of time. The same applies to messages - use the function for messages that delete themselves. This keeps communication discreet and reduces the risk of careless messages coming to light later.

9. always protect your mobile phone with a password and do not it home with youtake

A simple but often neglected step is to protect your mobile phone with a secure password. It's best to use biometric protection methods such as fingerprint or facial recognition, as these are harder to crack. Never take the second mobile phone you use for the affair into your home. Hide it in the car or leave it at work - this will minimise the risk of your partner discovering it.

10. only use old or publicly accessible images on dating portals

Avoid uploading recent pictures of yourself on dating platforms - and certainly not pictures that show you doing things together with your partner or family. Instead, use old pictures or pictures that are already publicly accessible, such as social media profile pictures. If someone discovers the pictures or approaches you about them, you can easily claim that the pictures have been stolen or that someone else has used your identity. This keeps your cover intact.

My promise to the "clever" among you

But I can promise you one thing right now: **Your affair will be discovered sooner or later.** No matter how careful you are, no matter how hard you try to hide everything. **We men are just too stupid to be skilful enough**

It's only a matter of time before you make a mistake - and believe me, it will happen. It starts with little things that we don't even notice at first. Sometimes it's a carelessly left message on a mobile phone, an inexplicable appointment or a thought that slips through in a weak moment and flashes up in a conversation with your partner.

The truth is that we can't keep it a perfect secret. Sooner or later, routine kills us, carelessness, or simply the fact that women are much more sensitive than we often want to admit. **They realise that something is wrong.** They may not be able to grasp it straight away, but this gut feeling makes them alert. This means that they will catch us at some point - not because they are watching our every move, but simply because they notice the change in our behaviour.

And what happens then? You can imagine the disaster. First the confrontation where you desperately try to deny it - but eventually the facts come out. The more you squirm, the worse it gets. **Every lie you build will eventually collapse like a house of cards.** Women have an incredible memory for details. They know exactly what you said and when, what excuse you used, why you're suddenly out so often in the evening. And if you think you can talk your way out of it, you'll soon realise that you're lost.

The truth is brutal: the affair not only destroys the trust in your relationship, but also puts you in a situation from which you cannot escape without damage. Because once you've been found out, it's almost impossible to completely rebuild trust. There is always this shadow hovering over the relationship. Every time you come home late or take your mobile phone into the bathroom, the doubt will return - and with it the question of whether you will do it again.

And believe me, this mistrust will not only wear your partner down, but also yourself. **You'll constantly feel like you're skating on thin ice.** Every little thing could give rise to suspicion again, and that can ruin the relationship in the long run. So before you jump into this game, remember that there are no winners. **In the end, both of you lose. So Buddy, cut the crap!**

The Hulk inside you - when the inner battle boils over

The myth of mood swings is true - and it is indeed a huge problem that creeps up on you until it takes over completely. For my part, I noticed it in my ever-shorter fuse and the sudden onset of aggression that spread like wildfire. And this despite the fact that Iactually awho needs harmony 'm person and always tries to be friendly and respectful. But if there's one thing that particularly triggers me, it's ignorant, cheeky and recklessly stupid people.

Especially those who think that the world only revolves around them - people who stomp through life without any consideration, without the slightest thought that their behaviour could disturb or hurt other people. It's these people, to whom the concept of "nurture" seems to be completely alien, who make my nerves fray.

One example that remains vividly in my memory: a man with dishevelled, long hair and baggy clothes that were far too baggy, who looked like a modern version of "Jesus Christ after the worm cure", walked past me.

On his hand was a small, filthy child whose condition fluctuated between adventure and neglect. The little girl looked like Pippi Longstocking after a particularly wild day, with a dirty face and torn clothes.

Of course, children deserve to play freely and carefree - there's no doubt about that. But letting your child run around the city completely neglected is another matter. There is something called a "wet wipe" and a change of clothes to get the child into a suitable condition after kindergarten if you are still going out in public. I see it with my own grandchildren - before they go to the ice cream parlour or the playground, they are freshened up and changed. Not out of vanity, but out of respect for the children themselves and the people around us.

This may sound harsh and perhaps even derogatory, but it is precisely at moments like this that the image of the eco-clientele is confirmed, which I cannot stand. These clichés may seem exaggerated, but they have their origins in real encounters like this one. It's particularly annoying when these types of people are the ones who point the finger and try to impose their world view on others as self-appointed moralisers. I'll say it openly: I find this hypocrisy disgusting.

On the other hand, these people don't seem to care how they look to others or what people think of them. That only makes me angrier - the arrogance with which they stylise themselves into moral messiah figures without having the decency to reflect on their own world. It's this attitude, this self-righteous ignorance, that makes my mood shoot from 0 to 100, as if someone had flicked the switch.

But now back to the story:

We are sitting in the outdoor area of the ice cream parlour, the Jesus guy with his child next to us, my wife opposite me. Suddenly the child stands up, lifts his little skirt, squats down and starts to wee - in public and where other people are sitting.

The guy didn't care at all. Instead of intervening, he just let the little girl carry on doing her business. It makes you wonder what kind of ignorant idiots there are, especially today when everyone has a mobile phone and could film something like that.

In short: the guy had disqualified himself as a father in every conceivable way. Let's call him, with his 50kg and his Mikado arms: "Jesus Christ after the worm cure".

My wife and I look at each other and can't believe it.

My wife then said to the guy calmly and reasonably: "Young man, there are toilets back there, that doesn't have to be..."

The Jesus guy replied: "Shut up, my child goes to pee where I want him to..."

Wrong answer, wrong tone, wrong time, wrong type, wrong to shit on my wife like that, wrong to weigh only 50 kilos and have Mikado arms, wrong to mess with me...

I got to him so quickly that he didn't even have time to get up. I gave the Jesus guy a good whack with the flat of my hand in front of his child.

I hadn't dared to use my fist, I didn't want him to fall apart like a Lego man. The guy flew over with his chair immediately.

I was amazed at the power of my punch. The guy then had all five of my fingerprints red on his face. The little girl was crying and screaming, in short: chaos to the power of ten.

My wife pulled on me and two male guests tried to me pull away . I then let go of the guy.from the Jesus guy

Somehow I immediately felt sorry, and I realised that this would not be without consequences. I could already see the first guests pulling out their mobile phones and making calls. We left the restaurant immediately and walked to the car park. It was around 500 metres away. We then drove home. When we got home, the police were already outside the house and five minutes later I was sitting in the green Minna, off to the police station.

I have no idea how they came across me and how they were able to get to us so quickly. I think some customer from the ice cream parlour must have followed us unnoticed and written down our car registration number.

Instead of a nice afternoon, I spent hours at the police station: calling a lawyer, waiting, questioning, accusations from my wife, an announcement from the lawyer, an announcement from the police.

We can no longer be seen in the ice cream parlour either, and all the neighbours now know that I'm the thug who beat up in front of his child. The trouble that followed was incredibly annoying and expensive: a big charge of assault, a big fine, the Jesus guy an annoying trial, a hefty lawyer's bill. And to top it all off, this eco-guy laughed cheekily in my face outside the courtroom.

I promised myself that this would never happen again. I even promised my wife. I wanted to stay calm from now on and never let myself be provoked by such eco arseholes again.

But things turned out differently. The Hulk in me broke out again and wanted to flatten people with his club...

It was the beginning of 2023, the heyday of these crazy and criminal climate glue idiots. They had been getting on my nerves for some time. It was unbelievable what was going on here in Berlin. I was stuck in traffic jams on my way to work almost every day. Ambulances and fire brigades couldn't get anywhere, people died because they couldn't be taken to hospital in time.

And the fact that these green arseholes were not held accountable annoyed me even more. I'm supposed to pay thousands of euros for a slap on the wrist? The climate fuzzies coerce people thousands of times, stop ambulances, people get killed and NOTHING happens to them???

In my eyes, something was going very wrong in this city. I felt it was wrong. Nevertheless, I resolved to stay calm and not attack any of these climate terrorists.

One Sunday in April, my daughter-in-law was pregnant and we wanted to take her to hospital because she wasn't feeling well.

Halfway there, nothing worked because of those fucking climate arseholes. Again those eco-wackos, who, as we now know, I had eaten to death...

If the book is too crass or offensive in places, I apologise. It was never my intention to hurt anyone or cause offence. My aim was to describe my experiences at the time as authentically as possible - raw, honest and unfiltered, as I felt them at the time. This also in-

cludes a somewhat coarse slang that some would describe as "Berlin redneck big mouth". This way of expressing myself is part of my background, it is direct, blunt and sometimes harsh.

I decided to keep this tone because I think it best conveys what I've been through. The feelings, the anger, the hurt - you can't always put all that into soft words. It wouldn't be real. In a life that is often full of complexity and contrasts, this direct language was reflected and it helped me to organise and process my emotions.

So if some passages seem too blunt or provocative, I ask for your understanding. Sometimes life is not just black and white, but loud, unruly and unembellished. It is important to me to tell the truth of my own story as I experienced it - not to shock, but to be honest. And sometimes that requires a bit more rough edges.

Especially after the incident with the guy in the ice cream parlour, I had nothing but pure hatred for all ecologists and green weirdos. At the beginning of 2023, the anger was boiling up inside me more and more, and I swore to myself that if anything happened to one of my family members because of these pissheads, I'd get the shit kicked out of me.

But back to the hospital action: I saw the climate stickers through the gap in the emergency lane. As always, I wanted to do it my way.

My son was driving, I jumped out of the passenger seat, ran about 150 metres between the cars to the sticky pissheads and kicked one of them directly in the face with a sideways kick without warning.

The colleague was knocked out immediately. I pulled the guy and another one off the street. The second guy started to fight back and I kicked him in the balls. Then he stopped resisting too.

The traffic was moving again and I was satisfied and had finally vented my anger.

I then ran a kilometre further in the direction of travel and got back into my son's car. To this day, nothing has come of the offence - I got away with it again. Because that would certainly NOT have ended with a fine. My son continued to berate me for hours because he couldn't believe how aggressive I was.

My daughter-in-law was really scared of me and I realised that I urgently needed help before I killed someone else.

The dissatisfaction with my life, the many negative experiences in my childhood and in recent years and the testosterone I had injected certainly played a role. Nevertheless, that is no excuse for my behaviour.

The crazy bloke had to change, go back to being the lovable guy he was in the 90s. I made up a few rules and changed my life fundamentally.

Never react immediately and impulsively again

I made a firm resolution to control my impulsive reactions. No more jumping into fight mode without first analysing the situation at . The motto was: close my eyes, take a deep breath and count to ten before I let myself get carried away. Easier said than done - I still have that warrior in me that whispers quietly: "Attack". But I no longer wanted to answer the call of anger.

So I started to stop reacting immediately to bad news. A simple trick that helped me was to set myself a time window of at least 24 hours. Only then did I allow myself to act. If a situation was complex, I preferred to think about it for a few days. My head was calmer this way, and my actions were more thoughtful, less impulsive.

Another important point was to seek advice from people I trust. Whether friends, family or colleagues - people who could help me make decisions with a clear head. This gave me more than a year of stable decisions and protected me from falling back into chaos.

Get professional help

Another step in my plan to regain control of my life was the appointment with a psychologist. I knew that I couldn't work through the old traumas from my childhood on my own. But the first attempt was a flop. The psychologist, an oddball, and I just couldn't connect. Even after the first session, I realised that it wasn't going to work. It didn't suit me, an otherwise open and extroverted person.

Maybe it wasn't the right time to let someone get so close to my deepest wounds. I decided to give myself the time I needed. But postponed was not cancelled - I firmly resolved to take the plunge again next year and tackle the shadows of the past.

Create a balance for your aggression

The next item on my list: Exercise to get rid of excess energy and pent-up aggression. Testosterone and adrenaline should be pumped out, and in the right way. Now I'm in a three-day rhythm: kick-boxing, strength training and endurance runs. The punching bag in my small home gym has already survived many of my bad days and has taken a beating in the process. This type of training is more than just fitness for me - it's therapy.

Find ways to relax and rest

The next big learning: consciously incorporating rest and relaxation into everyday life. My wife and I have developed our own little rituals that have brought us closer together. After work, we often go to the nearby lido. There we sit by the water with an Aperol in our hands, listen to the gentle waves and let the tension of the day roll off us. These little escapes from everyday life are like a short holiday for the soul.

Sometimes it's not about changing big things, but about creating the little moments of peace that help to promote positive thoughts. They are like little islands of calm in the often stormy sea of life.

Free yourself from ballast and negative influences

Another step in my transformation was to give up my self-employment. This decision was not an easy one, as I had been for over my own boss years. But it was precisely this point, the constant pressure, the juggling of orders and customer requests, that had brought me to the brink of madness. The decision to go back to work as an employee was like jumping in at the deep end - scary, yes, but also liberating.thirty

The six-month transition was tough, but the reward soon followed: a job in a company that became like a second home. Colleagues who made me feel welcome, exciting tasks and the knowledge that I would receive my salary at the end of the month without having to worry about it. The pressure was blown away. Today, when I talk to old acquaintances who are still self-employed, I hear about order slumps and existential fears. I then think: you did everything right.

My advice to anyone who finds themselves in a similar situation: Have the courage to rethink your life and get rid of any baggage. It takes strength, but as the old Indian proverb says: "When the horse is dead, get off."

Life is too short to keep going round in circles. Sometimes you have to stop, take a deep breath and change direction. These steps were my salvation - and maybe they can help you find your way to a better self too.

From now on, I immediately get rid of any ballast or things that annoy me. Why should I put myself through the stress? **If something doesn't fit, then get rid of it**

A small example: My old gym was just annoying. There was dirt everywhere, people who couldn't behave themselves and worn-out, dangerous equipment that was just waiting to send someone to hospital. **Every time I went to train there, I was annoyed.** It got to the point where I would go there in a bad mood - even though sport was supposed to be a way to relax.

So at some point I thought to myself: **Why are you still doing this?** Just because the contract was cheap? That's complete rubbish. So I pulled the ripcord and switched to another studio.

Brand new, real luxury - everything perfectly maintained, modern equipment, even a sauna. And the best thing: **no annoying people.** No crowds in the afternoon, no school brats letting off steam after class, just a pleasant, quiet atmosphere with people who really want to work out.

Sure, I'm now paying just under 100 euros a month, but you know what? **It's worth every cent.** Because now I really feel like going to the gym again. I'm looking forward to my time in the gym instead of avoiding it . And that's what counts: **Quality of life.** Sometimes you just have to be prepared to invest a little more in order to enjoy life again. Instead of getting worked up about little things that you could actually change quite easily. **Why wear yourself out unnecessarily when there are solutions?**

This applies to so many things in life. We simply have to get rid of things that stress us out or drain our energy. Whether it's the wrong fitness club, annoying acquaintances or habits that aren't good for you. **You only live once, and burdening yourself with baggage that you don't need to carry is a waste of time.**

Stop cheating - stay away from other women

No more escapades or extramarital "activities". I've banned anything that could trigger me, such as chubby, tattooed or red-haired ladies on Instagram or old contacts who might suddenly get in touch.

I destroyed all pictures and memories of my old flings. Also all phone numbers and Insta contacts.

My wife has the mobile phone pin, she can access my mobile phone at any time. That was also a real liberation, for example: one hundred per cent trust. I no longer have to worry that she'll discover something strange when she answers my mobile phone.

Because: a real man wets his wife's panties and not her eyes.

In this context, the film "The Perfect Secret" comes to mind. A group of friends are sitting together at dinner. One of the group comes up with the idea of putting their mobile phones on the table and seeing what messages come in.

Of course, a bunch of secrets and infidelities come out now. I couldn't have taken part in such a game when I was having an affair with

Isabell, then everything would have come to light much earlier. Back then, I was constantly getting messages from her, spiced up with explicit pictures of her body parts.

Today I could put my mobile phone on the table with complete peace of mind - it would be silent.

Tell the truth, rarely make promises

No more lies. I no longer lie to my wife or anyone else. If I'm asked, I tell the truth.

That was also a learning process, because you also have to learn to live with the consequences if you "mess up". No more white lies or twisted truths either.

A promise is now also a promise. I now consider several times and carefully whether I can keep a promise. If I realise beforehand that I can't fulfil it, I don't make a promise.

However, you also need to communicate exactly why you are not willing to make a promise, for example. People usually understand if you explain it in detail.

This has greatly improved my relationship with my wife, family, friends and colleagues. I am now perceived as a reliable man who keeps his word. The second positive effect: I no longer have to re-member so much and what I told whom and when. Lies eventually come out.

We men are daft anyway and will blab at some point. If you don't lie, you'll live a calmer life. Sure, it's sometimes hard when you've mes-sed up and you know in advance that your sweetheart will definitely be angry. No matter - in any case, the thunder won't be as big as if a lie comes out afterwards.

Promises are the same issue. Don't make promises that you know in advance you can't possibly keep. Not even because you want to please someone or because of a "good mood". If you can't keep your promise, for whatever reason, even if you didn't mean it in a bad way, you will be perceived as an unreliable liar. Is that what you want? No, no man wants that.

A simple mechanism: ask yourself beforehand whether it is possible and whether you feel like making a promise or commitment at all. I see a promise like a loan agreement. You ask yourself beforehand whether you can even afford the instalments. You make comparisons, get quotes and only then make a decision. So treat a promise in the same way

Hair loss in men - Why your charisma counts more than your hair

Hair loss in men is an issue that concerns many, especially when the first signs of a receding hairline or thinning patches appear on the head. For many men, hair is a symbol of youth, vitality and self-confidence. But what happens when the mirror suddenly tells a different story? There are times when you get the feeling that losing your hair also means losing your attractiveness. But that is far from the case.

Fortunately, I am still blessed with a full head of hair and, at the age of 57, I don't have a single grey hair. My grandfather and my father also had a full head of hair with only a few grey strands until they were very old. I think this is a gift from my genes, for which I am very grateful. I also do a lot of sport, don't smoke and rarely drink alcohol, which certainly contributes to my appearance. People often think I'm years younger, which is flattering, but also shows that a healthy lifestyle can do more than you think.

But back to the subject of hair loss: my second eldest son, at 27, already has a few grey hairs. This shows me that heredity plays a decisive role in hair loss, but it is by no means the only factor. Stress, hormones and health issues can also play their part.

But why does charisma count more than hair? It's simple: hair loss can change your outward appearance, but it's your inner glow that really counts. People are attracted to confidence, humour, intelligence and the way you present yourself. There are countless examples of men who have an irrepressible charisma despite - or perhaps because of - their baldness. From Bruce Willis to Jason Statham - their heads may be bald, but their presence fills any room. Hair loss can be a sign of the natural ageing process, but it's not the end of your self-confidence.

So what can you do if you notice that your hair is thinning? Firstly, accept it and try to take it in your stride. It's important to realise that hair loss doesn't have to affect your abilities, charisma or attractiveness. Your attitude, your smile and how you interact with other people make much more of a difference. Secondly, if you want it, there are treatments that can help slow or conceal hair loss - from special shampoos and medications to hair transplants. But the most important thing is that you feel comfortable in your own skin.

Because at the end of the day, those around you won't love you because of your hair, but because of your personality, your energy and the memories you share with them. And that's exactly the point: your charisma is what makes you unique. Whether you have a full head of hair or are bald - be the person who othersinspires and makes them feel good. And remember: a man is not defined by his hair, but by what he does with his life.

Causes of hair loss

Androgenetic alopecia (hereditary hair loss): The most common cause of hair loss in men is androgenetic alopecia, also known as male pattern baldness. It is genetic and is the effect of caused by , a breakdown product of testosterone. **dihydrotestosterone (DHT)**

DHT causes the **hair follicles to shrink** and the hair to become thinner and thinner until it finally falls out.

Hormonal changes: Hormonal fluctuations, particularly an imbalance of testosterone and its derivatives, can also cause hair loss. These changes often occur in connection with the ageing process.

Stress and psychological strain: High levels of stress and emotional strain can lead to a condition called telogen effluvium, in which a large number of hairs enter the resting phase at the same time and fall out.

Nutritional deficiencies: A lack of essential nutrients such as iron, zinc, vitamin D and proteins can promote hair loss. An unbalanced diet impairs the health of the hair follicles.

Diseases and medication: Certain diseases such as thyroid disorders, diabetes and autoimmune diseases as well as medication (e.g. chemotherapy) can trigger hair loss.

Lifestyle and environmental factors: Smoking, excessive alcohol consumption and environmental pollution can have a negative impact on hair health.

Measures against hair loss

Drug treatment:

Minoxidil: A topical medication that is applied directly to the scalp and can stimulate hair growth. It is available over the counter and is often used as a first treatment option.

Finasteride: A prescription medication that blocks the conversion of testosterone into DHT. It can slow down and partially reverse hair loss.

Hair transplantation: A surgical method in which hair follicles are transplanted from densely overgrown areas (often from the back of the head) into bald or sparsely haired areas. Modern techniques such as FUE (Follicular Unit Extraction) offer natural results with minimal scarring.

I often see men who have undergone a hair transplant, especially on holiday in Turkey. They can usually be recognised by a turban-like head bandage. The largest clinics specialising in FUE are located in Istanbul. There is already a lot of advertising at Istanbul airport.

Last year, I struck up a conversation with a young man from Cologne at Istanbul airport. The young man said he was 35 years old and had undergone treatment at Elithair.

He told me that 5,000 follicles were removed from the back of his head and implanted three days later. The follicles are probably grown in a nutrient solution. The whole procedure probably takes seven days and he paid around 3,000 euros. If I remember correctly, the removal and transplantation of a follicle costs 1.70 euros.

Laser therapy: Low-dose laser therapy (LLLT) can improve blood circulation to the scalp and promote hair growth. This method is non-invasive and can be carried out both at home and in specialised clinics.

Lifestyle changes:

Diet: A balanced diet, rich in vitamins and minerals, supports the health of the hair follicles. Foods such as green leafy vegetables, nuts, fish and eggs are particularly beneficial.

Stress management: Techniques such as yoga, meditation and regular exercise can help to reduce stress and thus prevent stress-related hair loss.

Care products:

Shampoos and conditioners: Special products containing ingredients such as biotin, caffeine and ketoconazole can improve scalp health and slow down hair loss.

Hair oils and serums: Products with natural oils such as rosemary oil, peppermint oil and castor oil can promote blood circulation to the scalp and support hair growth.

The new ideal image of the man - masculinity in the 21st century

The image of the 'classic' man has been deeply engrained in our cultural consciousness for generations. Strength, independence, assertiveness and status as the provider of the family - these were the core characteristics of masculinity for a long time. But modern society is changing rapidly, and with it the ideal image of the man. For men going through the menopause, this change often poses a challenge. In a phase in which many are already struggling with questions of identity and self-worth, the change in gender roles creates additional uncertainty.

But what does masculinity really mean in the 21st century? Moving away from traditional role models towards a more versatile, flexible understanding of masculinity - this is the direction in which society is moving. The question is: as a man, how can you going through the menopausenot only accept this change, but also see it as an opportunity to redefine yourself?

Saying goodbye to old role models

The idea of the "typical" man - strong, emotionless and always in control mode - is no longer up to date. These role models date back to a time when men had to provide for their families financially and were often not allowed to show any emotional weakness. This traditional definition of masculinity has characterised many generations and has been accepted unquestioningly by most men.

However, this image has changed considerably in recent decades. Nowadays, men are no longer defined solely by their professional successes or their role as providers. Social changes, the strengthening of women's rights and the softening of rigid gender roles have led to the old image of men being increasingly questioned. It is no longer just financial stability or physical strength that defines a man, but also his ability to be emotional, share his worries and cultivate a deeper connection with his fellow human beings.

For many men going through the menopause, who are still strongly characterised by traditional role models, this change is a challenge. The image of the "tough man" who has a solution for everything and shows no weakness no longer fits in with modern times. Men are faced with the task of rethinking their identity - and this in a phase of life that is already characterised by many uncertainties.

A more versatile understanding of masculinity

Modern masculinity is no longer monolithic. Instead, today it is about allowing different facets of one's own personality. Emotionality, empathy and vulnerability are no longer weaknesses, but important aspects of a mature and reflective masculinity. Men today are allowed to be more themselves , they are allowed to show their worries and fears without being seen as "weak".

During the menopause, when many men feel that they are no longer at their professional or physical peak, this new ideal can be a relief. There is room for honesty - towards oneself and others. Men are allowed to admit that they don't always have to be strong, that they have doubts or feel overwhelmed. Accepting emotions and admitting weakness are key components of healthy masculinity today.

This new understanding of masculinity also offers the opportunity to free oneself from excessive expectations. Men no longer have to be the tireless "doers" who have everything under control. They are allowed to make mistakes, they are allowed to pause and ask themselves what they really want. It is a departure from an ideal that has often put men under pressure - in favour of a self-image that leaves more room for individuality and self-acceptance.

The role of relationships

As the male ideal changes, so do the relationships between men and their partners, families and friends. Partnerships today are no longer based on a clear role structure in which the man is the provider and the woman is the emotional support. Instead, equality, respect and a shared understanding of responsibility take centre stage.

For men going through the menopause, this means that they can learn to be more open and honest in their relationships. They no longer have to play the role of the silent "rock in the surf" who wants to solve all problems alone. Instead, they can allow themselves to talk about their feelings and accept support from their partner. This kind of emotional closeness and communication can strengthen a partnership and give it a new, deeper quality.

Friendships between men are also changing. The idea that men are only allowed to talk about sport, work or superficial topics is increasingly giving way to a culture in which there is also room for more in-depth conversations. Men are allowed to support each other without fear of being seen as "soft" or "unmanly". These kinds of open and honest friendships can be a valuable resource, especially during the menopause.

Masculinity as a personal expression

Another important aspect of modern masculinity is the realisation that every man can express it in his own way. There is no longer one right image of a man. Instead, it's about finding out what makes sense for each individual and what values and goals he wants to pursue in his life.

For men in the menopause, who often go through a phase of self-reflection, this freedom can be liberating. Instead of continuing to cling to outdated ideas, they can find their own way of living masculinity - be it through new hobbies, professional reorientation or discovering emotional sides that were previously hidden.

Friends or mates from the perspective of an ego type

In the past, I couldn't imagine really engaging with other people - the thought of making commitments or even being emotionally dependent felt constricting to me. I always saw myself as an independent spirit, going my own way without being dependent on others. This was also because I have always been able to cope well on my own. Even in the times when my life was chaotic and restless, I dealt with myself and managed without others.

I also don't fit the image of the "typical man" who enthusiastically follows every football match or swears by Formula 1. That was never my thing. I'm the type who prefers to go out into nature, indulge in action-packed hobbies or spend the weekend at the lake. My wife has always appreciated that about me - for her, a football fan who's always in the pub shouting with the lads was never an option. She always said that I was interesting to her because I had a mind of my own and didn't conform to the cliché.

The mistrust of other people has become deeply rooted in me - it is no coincidence. Sure, there were good moments in my childhood, but the negative experiences were more deeply ingrained. I learned early on that other people often pursued their own agendas, and so I developed an image of the world that was more geared towards defence and self-protection. Of course, as a child and teenager I had a few friends, real friendships, the kind you make in your youth - uncomplicated, easy and without ulterior motives. But after reunification and my move to Berlin, these relationships broke down. In the big, impersonal city, I quickly realised that friendships in adulthood were often different.

I was very successful in my career and this attracted people who, as I later realised, were less interested in me as a person. It was my success, my position and my financial security that fascinated them. More and more often, new acquaintances turned out to be "friends" who wanted to share in my success - no more and no less. The conversations only centred on what I had, what I could achieve and how I was leading my life. There was no real depth, no connection. How many times did I sit at a meeting and feel like I was just a stepping stone for them?

That shaped my behaviour: I began to play a role in friendships, just as I did in relationships with women. I played at friendship, was charming and approachable, made small talk and seemed interested. But in reality, I never let anyone toget close me, always kept a certain distance and was always on the go inside. Instead of making real connections, I built walls around myself. Sometimes I realised how isolated I actually was, but the disappointments of the past made it hard for me to do anything else.

But over time, something changed in me. Perhaps it was the sum of these superficial friendships or the realisation that I myself was contributing to not letting anyone get close to me. In recent years, with my new phase of life, I began to question this mistrust. I slowly allowed people to get closer to me again, learnt that not everyone sees a benefit in friendship and that there are people who mean it honestly. It's been a long road, and sometimes I'm still sceptical. But I have learnt that real connections enrich life and that maybe it's time to give the world and people a second chance.

But this independence also came at a price: without real friendships to hold up a mirror and tell you when you were wrong, I often got stuck in my own cycle of thoughts. There were "mates" for paintballing, action days, hunting or wakeboarding, and I enjoyed spending time with them. But they were more like acquaintances - I was happy when I saw them, but I didn't miss them when weeks or months went by.

Only now, with my new attitude, do I recognise the value of deeper relationships. My 'polarity reversal', as I call it, has opened my eyes. I have become calmer, a little more relaxed and, above all, I now appreciate things that I would have previously dismissed as unnecessary baggage. Thanks to my wife and my changed perspective, I was able to experience how real friendships enrich, how they offer support and give you a different perspective.

It's a completely new experience for me to have a relaxed chat and a beer with friends without my mind being restless or already moving on to the next destination. It used to be all about success and independence, about my own pleasure. Today, I realise that family, friends and genuine togetherness give me a sense of satisfaction that I never knew before.

I now see how real friendships give you a lot and at the same time show you that you have to give back just as much - and that this is often the true meaning of a friendship. Now it's not just the activities we do together that I enjoy. It's the honest togetherness, the laughter, the conversations and the feeling that someone is there when the going gets tough. It's a new way of life that I could never have imagined before - and today I wouldn't want to do without it.

The power of male hormones: an in-depth look at their effects

In this chapter, I would like to highlight some biological principles that can be helpful in better understanding your own behaviour and physical changes during the menopause. This is because the role of hormones - especially male hormones such as testosterone and DHT - is often underestimated, even though they are crucial for our well-being.

The main players: testosterone and dihydrotestosterone (DHT)

Testosterone, the "male hormone" par excellence, is mainly produced in the testicles, but also to a lesser extent in the adrenal glands. Testosterone is responsible for what makes us appear typically male: Beard growth, the deeper voice, pronounced muscle mass, strong bones. But its effect goes far beyond this - our libido, sperm production and even our mood are also influenced by this substance. In a way, it is the engine that drives us and gives us the energy we need.

DHT, a degradation product of testosterone, is also of great importance, even if it is less active. This hormone is partly responsible for the typical male pattern baldness. A blessing and a curse at the same time, because the same hormone that makes our beard sprout when we are young can lead to thinning hair in old age.

The effect on our body

Sexual development and reproduction: Without testosterone, we would not develop the characteristics typical of men. It contributes to the development of our sexual characteristics as early as the prenatal phase. It ensures that we later develop a strong physique, body hair and a deeper voice. During puberty, testosterone virtually takes over and shapes us into what we perceive as men - from the splendour of our hair to our height.

Muscle and bone mass: It is not for nothing that testosterone is considered a natural anabolic. It supports muscle growth and strengthens bones, protects us from osteoporosis in old age and promotes a healthy, stable body structure. At best, we get a good foundation that enables us to feel strong and fit later in life.

Metabolism and body fat: This is where it gets particularly interesting for those of us who are wondering about the tummy bulge that has so secretly and quietly spread over the years. Testosterone ensures that our body can burn fat efficiently and maintain more muscle mass. When we are young, this works like clockwork - but when testosterone levels drop, this mechanism changes and suddenly the body stores fat rather than burning it.

Mental health: Testosterone also influences our psyche more than many people realise. Studies show that men with low testosterone levels are more prone to mood swings, depression and listlessness. Our ability to concentrate decreases and we notice that we find it difficult to motivate ourselves or stay focussed. During the menopause, these symptoms can intensify and we feel that we are no longer really "in control".

Hormonal imbalances - when testosterone levels get out of balance

A balanced hormone balance is crucial for our well-being and health. However, if this balance starts to falter, a wide range of problems can arise that have both physical and mental effects. Let's take a look at how an imbalance of male hormones can affect our body:

Hypogonadism

Hypogonadism describes a condition in which the body does not produce enough testosterone. This can be distressing for affected men as it leads to a number of unpleasant symptoms, including

- **Decreased libido.**: The interest in sexuality and the ability to feel sexual reactions often diminish

- **Reduced energy:** General energy and vitality can decrease significantly, leading to permanent fatigue.

- **Loss of muscle and bone mass:** Testosterone is important for maintaining muscle mass and bone density. A deficiency can therefore lead to weaker bones and a loss of muscle strength.

Hypogonadism can be very stressful both physically and mentally. Fortunately, this condition can often be treated well with testosterone replacement therapy, which can bring testosterone levels to a healthy level and thus significantly improve quality of life.

Hypergonadism

While hypogonadism is characterised by a testosterone level that is too low, hypergonadism describes the exact opposite - namely an excessively high testosterone level. This excess can also have a negative effect:

- **Aggressiveness**: A high testosterone level can lead to uncontrollable outbursts of anger and strong irritability.

- **Acne:** Excessive testosterone production can stimulate sebaceous gland activity, which often leads to skin problems such as acne.

- **Enlarged prostate:** A permanent overproduction of testosterone can lead to an enlarged prostate, which can make urination difficult.

- **Infertility**: An excessively high testosterone level can have a negative effect on sperm production and thus impair fertility.

Other hormonal disorders

Other hormonal disorders can also affect the testosterone level and thus the balance of the hormone balance:

- **Polycystic ovary syndrome (PCOS):** Although this syndrome occurs in women, it is a good example of how excess testosterone can cause problems - in women these include symptoms such as irregular menstruation, increased body hair and infertility.

- **Hormone-producing tumours:** In rare cases, a tumour can increase the production of testosterone and lead to a variety of hormone-related symptoms.

Knowledge about these disorders can be helpful in a better understanding of the influence of our hormones on our healthdeveloping and well-being. Changes in testosterone levels often affect us more than we realise. A balanced hormone balance is therefore a key to a healthy and fulfilling life.

Bioidentical hormones

Bioidentical hormones have attracted a lot of attention in recent years, particularly as an alternative to conventional hormone replacement therapies. These hormones are often seen as a natural option as their molecular structure is the same as that produced by the body itself. In this article, we will take an in-depth look at bioidentical hormones, discuss their relevance to hormone therapy and discuss potential advantages and disadvantages.

What are bioidentical hormones?

Bioidentical hormones are hormones whose chemical structure corresponds to that of the hormones produced naturally by the human body. In contrast, synthetic hormones are made by producing chemical compounds that have similar, but not identical, structures to natural hormones. Bioidentical hormones are often derived from plant extracts such as wild yams or soya and then converted into hormone preparations in laboratories.

Use of bioidentical hormones

Bioidentical hormones are often used for hormone replacement therapy (HRT), especially in women during the menopause or in men with low testosterone levels. In women, bioidentical oestrogens, progesterone and testosterone can be used to relieve symptoms such as hot flushes, insomnia, vaginal dryness and mood swings. In men, testosterone replacement therapy with bioidentical testosterone can be used to treat symptoms such as reduced libido, fatigue and muscle weakness.

Advantages and disadvantages of bioidentical hormones

Bioidentical hormones are often seen as a safer alternative to synthetic hormones as their molecular structure is similar to the natural hormone. Proponents argue that bioidentical hormones are better accepted and metabolised by the body, leading to a lower likelihood of side effects. In addition, the individualisation of hormone therapy through bioidentical hormones can help to more precisely control and adjust an individual's hormone levels.

On the other hand, there are also concerns about the safety and efficacy of bioidentical hormones. Some studies have shown that bioidentical hormones may have similar risks to synthetic hormones, particularly in relation to the risk of breast cancer and cardiovascular disease in women. In addition, bioidentical hormones can be more expensive than synthetic hormones and may not be covered by all insurance plans.

Decabolin and steroids: stay away from the devil's stuff

Decabolin, also known as nandrolone decanoate, is a synthetic anabolic steroid commonly used by bodybuilders and athletes to build muscle mass and increase performance. It belongs to the class of anabolic steroids, which are man-made variants of the male sex hormone testosterone. While some people advocate their use to improve athletic performance, there are significant risks and potential side effects, especially if they are abused or taken without medical supervision. The fact is that you gain a lot of weight in a short space of time. For me it was 30 kilograms within six weeks. However, I stuffed everything into me, ate constantly and went to the gym almost every day.

Mechanism of action of Decabolin and other steroids

Decabolin and other anabolic steroids work by binding to androgen receptors in the body and increasing protein synthesis and nitrogen retention. This leads to an acceleration of muscle building and an improvement in regeneration after training. In addition, steroids can also stimulate the metabolism and increase fat burning, resulting in an improved physique.

Effects on the male body

Muscle mass and strength: One of the main reasons for using Decabolin and other steroids is to increase muscle mass and strength. By increasing protein synthesis, they help to build muscle faster and increase performance.

Improved recovery: Steroids can shorten the recovery time after training by accelerating the regeneration of muscle tissue. This allows athletes to perform more intense training programmes and recover faster from injuries.

Metabolic stimulation: Anabolic steroids can speed up the metabolism, leading to increased fat burning and an improved physique. This can be particularly beneficial for bodybuilders who are aiming for a low body fat percentage.

Risks and side effects

Despite their potential benefits, Decabolin and other steroids carry significant health risks, especially when misused or used without medical supervision. Possible side effects include:

Cardiovascular diseases: Steroid use can lead to an increase in blood pressure, elevated cholesterol levels and an increased risk of heart attacks and strokes. I can tell you a thing or two about that.

For 5 years now, after using Deca several times, I have had to take blood pressure tablets.

Increased susceptibility to infections. I realised for myself that I definitely had to deal with colds much more often. Probably also because I went to the gym too often. McFit can't exactly be described as clean, it's easy to catch something there. At least that's the case at my gym in Berlin Lichterfelde.

Hormonal imbalances: Taking steroids can disrupt the natural hormonal balance and lead to problems such as gynaecomastia (enlarged mammary glands in men), testicular atrophy (shrinkage of the testicles) and impotence.

Psychological effects: Steroids can lead to mood swings, aggression, depression and psychotic symptoms known as "roid rage". I described these symptoms in detail in the previous section.

Liver damage: Oral use of steroids can stress the liver and lead to liver damage, including liver inflammation and liver tumours.

Infections at the injection site. As soon as you do not use proper syringe material or disinfect it insufficiently, the risk of infection at the injection site is pre-programmed and very unpleasant. Often only an antibiotic will help.

Ugly acne pimples. If you take anabolic steroids in the gym, you can quickly see it: fat pimples on your back, on your head and especially around your triceps. The first time I experienced this effect myself, I just thought: "Oh you...!" I suddenly had pimples on my scalp and back. For someone like me, who normally never has a single pimple, it was like a shock. My skin is naturally smooth and well-groomed - women often admired me for it. Perhaps this was also due to the fact that I had neurodermatitis as a child and always had to take special care of my skin.

Over the years, this has become something of a ritual. Now, at 57, my skin looks great, almost like someone in their mid-forties. These spots stood out like a red rag - for me and for others too. Fortunately, they disappeared when I stopped taking steroids.

Vitamins and nutrition - how to stay in balance

Natural foods not only provide the energy we need, but also the vitamins and nutrients our bodies need to function optimally. Vitamins play a crucial role in numerous biochemical processes, from energy production to cell regeneration. They can also boost the immune system, improve skin health and even influence mood.

One of the most important vitamins is vitamin C, which is essential for the immune system. It is a powerful antioxidant that fights free radicals and protects cells from damage. Vitamin C is mainly found in fresh fruit such as oranges, lemons, kiwis and papayas, but also in vegetables such as broccoli, peppers and kale.

Vitamin D is another essential vitamin, often referred to as the 'sunshine vitamin', as the body produces it through exposure to sunlight on the skin. It plays an important role in the maintenance of bone health, the regulation of the

calcium metabolism and strengthening the immune system. Foods such as oily fish, eggs and fortified foods are good sources of vitamin D.

B vitamins, including B1, B2, B3, B5, B6, B7, B9 and B12, are critical for a variety of functions in the body, including energy metabolism, cell division and neurotransmitter production. They are found in a variety of foods, including meat, fish, eggs, dairy products, wholemeal products, pulses and green leafy vegetables.

In addition to vitamins, melatonin is another interesting molecule that is often discussed in relation to nutrition and health. Melatonin is a hormone produced in the pineal gland of the brain and plays a key role in regulating the sleep-wake cycle. It is often taken as a dietary supplement to treat sleep disorders or to combat jet lag. In addition, melatonin is also valued for its antioxidant properties and there is evidence that it can support the immune system and promote brain health.

It is important to note that a balanced diet rich in various nutrients is the best source of vitamins and minerals. While supplements can be helpful in some cases, they should not be considered a substitute for a healthy diet. A varied and balanced diet rich in fresh fruits, vegetables, whole grains, lean protein and healthy fats provides the nutrients our bodies need to function optimally and stay healthy.

A balanced diet plan is important for people of all ages and lifestyles, especially for a man over 50 who has an office job and may lead a sedentary lifestyle. Here is an example of a sensible eating plan:

Breakfast:

Oatmeal with fresh fruit (e.g. bananas, berries) and a spoonful of linseed or chia seeds for fibre and omega-3 fatty acids.

A glass of low-fat milk or almond milk for calcium and vitamin D.

A handful of unsalted nuts (e.g. almonds, walnuts) for healthy fats and proteins.

Lunch:

Grilled chicken or salmon with a portion of quinoa or wholegrain rice and steamed vegetables (e.g. broccoli, carrots, spinach) for protein, fibre and vitamins.

A mixed green salad with tomatoes, cucumber and a light vinaigrette on the side for extra nutrients and fibre.

Snack (between meals):

Greek yoghurt with honey and a handful of berries for protein, probiotics and antioxidants.

Vegetable sticks (e.g. carrots, peppers, celery) with hummus or guacamole as a healthy and nutritious snack.

Dinner:

Baked or grilled vegetables (e.g. courgette, aubergine, mushrooms) with a small portion of wholemeal pasta or potatoes for fibre and complex carbohydrates.

A piece of lean meat (e.g. chicken breast, turkey fillet) or fish (e.g. salmon, trout) as a source of protein.

A glass of water or herbal tea to hydrate and aid digestion.

Before going to bed (optional):

A cup of low-fat yoghurt or a glass of almond milk for a light, protein-rich meal that stabilises blood sugar levels and promotes sleep.

It is important to ensure adequate hydration, so men should drink water regularly throughout the day (3 litres is recommended). In addition, he can adjust his meals as needed and adapt to his individual preferences and nutritional needs to ensure optimal health and well-being.

Sport and exercise - the best medicine for ageing men

If there is one thing we men should not underestimate as we get older, it is the impact of **sport and exercise** on our physical and mental well-being. It's no secret that as we get older, our bodies are no longer as efficient as they were in our 20s or 30s. Muscle mass decreases, metabolism slows down and joints suddenly make themselves felt when we stand up. But instead of accepting this as an inevitable fate, we have it in our own hands to counteract it - and **sport is the best medicine** we can prescribe ourselves.

Why sport is so important in old age

Regular exercise is not only good for the body, but also for the mind. **Exercise reduces stress, improves mood and helps to avoid depressive moods**, which can occur in many men during the menopause. But it's not just about mental well-being. Physical activity strengthens the cardiovascular system, promotes muscle development and helps to keep the joints flexible. And let's be honest: who wants to lose weight prematurely in old age? **We want to stay fit, feel good and be able to continue to actively enjoy life.**

Another important point: **sport helps to stabilise testosterone levels.** The hormone level drops in many men during the menopause, which can lead to tiredness, listlessness and a general decline in performance. However, regular exercise stimulates testosterone production - and this has a direct impact on libido, energy levels and general well-being. **In short: if you exercise, you stay more masculine.**

Which sports are best for men in old age?

In principle, it's not about choosing a particular sport, but about finding something that you can do regularly and that you enjoy. **Strength training** is ideal for maintaining muscle mass and strengthening the body. As men age, they tend to lose muscle mass, which leads to weakness and an increased risk of injury. **Regular strength training prevents this.**

Endurance sports such as running, cycling or swimming are excellent for strengthening the cardiovascular system and increasing stamina. If you need to protect your joints, you should opt for swimming or cycling to take the strain off your knees and hips.also

Flexibility training, such as yoga or stretching, is a good addition to other sports. As we get older, our muscles and joints become stiffer. Stretching exercises help to maintain flexibility and prevent injuries.

Sport as a social factor

Another positive aspect of sport is the **social factor**. Many men tend to withdraw socially as they get older. However, those who exercise regularly, be it at the gym or in a group running, swimming or cycling, automatically socialise with like-minded people. This not only promotes physical health, but also mental health, as social ties become increasingly important in old age.

3-split training plan for men

To really benefit from effective strength training and train all muscle groups, a **3-split training plan** is an excellent choice. This plan splits the training into three sessions spread over the week. Training is done every other day, which provides enough recovery time for the body to recover between workouts. The focus is on training each muscle group intensively once a week.

Day 1: Chest, shoulder, triceps

Bench press (barbell or dumbbell) 4 sets of 8-12 repetitions The bench press is one of the best exercises for strengthening the chest muscles. The stabilising muscles in the shoulders and arms are also trained.

Incline bench press (dumbbell or barbell) 3 sets of 8-12 repetitions This exercise focusses more on the upper part of the chest muscles.

Side raises (dumbbells) 3 sets of 10-15 repetitions For the shoulders, side raises are an isolated exercise that targets the middle deltoid muscle.

Shoulder press (dumbbell or machine) 3 sets of 8-12 repetitions Here the entire shoulder area is activated, especially the front and side shoulders.

Tricep press on the cable pulley 3 sets of 10-12 repetitions An isolated exercise that targets the triceps.

Overhead tricep press with dumbbells 3 sets of 8-10 repetitions .This exercise is ideal for training the long head of the triceps

Day 2: Back, biceps

Deadlift 4 sets of 6-8 repetitions One of the most important basic exercises that trains the lower back, the gluteal muscles and the back of the thighs. It strengthens the entire back and promotes stability.

Lat pull-ups (or pull-ups) 3 sets of 8-12 repetitions
This exercise focusses on the broad back muscle (latissimus) and
creates a wider back.

Rowing on the cable pulley 3 sets of 8-12 repetitions
Rowing is a great exercise for the middle back and the back muscles
along the spine.

One-arm dumbbell row 3 sets of 8-12 repetitions
A very effective exercise to strengthen the muscles in the upper back
and shoulders.

Barbell curls (biceps) 3 sets of 8-12 repetitions
A basic exercise for the biceps that trains both the short and long
head of the biceps.

Hammer curls with dumbbells 3 sets of 10-12 repetitions
This exercise not only strengthens the biceps, but also the brachialis
muscle, which is responsible for the thickness of the arm.

Day 3: Legs, stomach

Squats (barbell) 4 sets of 8-10 repetitions
One of the best full-body exercises that trains the thighs, buttocks
and lower back in particular.

Leg press 3 sets of 8-12 repetitions
An alternative exercise to the squat to specifically strengthen the
legs.

Leg extension (machine) 3 sets of 10-15 repetitions
Isolated exercise focussing on the quadriceps.

Leg curl (machine) 3 sets of 10-15 repetitions
This exercise targets the back of the thighs and the buttocks.

Calf raises (standing or sitting) 4 sets of 12-15 repetitions For the
calf muscles, which are often neglected by many men.

Crunches (abdominals) 3 sets of 15-20 repetitions
Standard exercise for the abdomen to strengthen the straight abdominal muscles.

Plank (forearm support) 3 sets of 30-60 seconds each
An excellent exercise for the entire core muscles and stability.

Summary:

This **3-split training plan** is perfect for men who want to exercise regularly and cover all muscle groups. It ensures that the body is sufficiently challenged, but also has enough time to regenerate - which is extremely important, especially as we get older. **Regular sport and exercise are the best medicine for us men** to stay fit, strong and healthy in old age.

Dr Steiger comes - Luck at , or why men are afraid of a urologist

My goodness, I was terrified of the urologist. My wife wouldn't let up, she kept reminding me to finally make an appointment. Stupid as I was, I refused - the idea of another man fiddling with my arse was simply unpleasant. I had completely ignored the fact that such behaviour could lead to any illnesses remaining undetected.

Shortly before Covid, she had had enough and took the initiative herself. Without asking me, she made appointments with the urologist and internist. She didn't do this to annoy me - on the contrary, she was worried and wanted to make sure I was healthy. Fortunately, there were no abnormalities at either examination.

The best thing about these appointments? I finally had the opportunity to speak openly with my doctor about various issues that I had been putting off for ages. I addressed issues that had always made me uncomfortable - and that I had never really taken seriously.

Looking back, I should have tackled all of this much earlier. The feeling of finally being able to talk openly about health concerns was indescribably relieving. It wasn't just about physical health, but also about clearing my head and finding more inner peace. These conversations with the doctor not only took away my fear of the examinations themselves, but also my reluctance to talk openly about my concerns. I felt like I was finally in control of my health and realised how important regular check-ups are - for me and for my family.

Today, I see these visits to the doctor as one of the best decisions I have made for myself and my loved ones. I have realised that taking responsibility for your health is not a sign of weakness, but of strength.

Why men should pay attention to prostate and bowel cancer screening ?

Health is a precious commodity that is often neglected, especially by men. We tend to take care of others before we think about ourselves. But now is the time to change that. As men, we need to take responsibility for our health, and an important step in this is regular screening, especially for prostate and bowel cancer.

Why are these examinations important?

Prostate and bowel cancer are two of the most common types of cancer in men. Although they often occur in old age, they can affect men of any age. The tricky thing about these cancers is that they often cause no symptoms in the early stages. This means that they can develop unnoticed until they are more advanced and harder to treat.

The role of preventive medical check-ups

The good news is that both prostate and bowel cancer can be detected early if men have regular screening tests. For prostate cancer, this usually includes a digital rectal examination (DRU) and a prostate-specific antigen (PSA) test. These tests are quick, simple and can save lives by detecting potential signs of cancer even before symptoms appear.

For bowel cancer, colonoscopy is the gold standard for screening. Although many men may shy away from this test, it is important to understand that it is painless and can potentially be life-saving. By removing polyps during the colonoscopy, doctors can significantly reduce the risk of colon cancer.

Why do men hesitate to have themselves examined?

Many men are reluctant to have an examination for fear of the unknown or out of a sense of shame. But we must not neglect our health for fear of discomfort or embarrassment. The truth is that a brief discomfort during the examination is a small price to pay for our health.

Prostate and men's health - The thing with the taboo

Okay, guys, now it's getting serious. The prostate. This small, inconspicuous thing that we would prefer to ignore for as long as possible. But here's the truth: sooner or later it comes into focus. And if we're honest, most of us know frighteningly little about it. So, let's buckle up and take a closer look.

What does the prostate actually do?

The prostate is a small gland, about the size of a walnut, and sits directly under the bladder. Its main job? It produces part of the seminal fluid. More precisely, it ensures that the sperm have enough "fuel" to make the journey on their way out. Without a prostate - no offspring. But even if family planning is no longer an issue, the prostate still has an important function. It regulates the flow of urine by surrounding the urethra. Sounds harmless? It is - until it starts to cause stress.

Why does the prostate grow with age?

Here comes the thing that affects us all at some point: as we get older, the prostate tends to get bigger. This phenomenon is called **benign prostatic hyperplasia (BPH)** - don't panic, it's not dangerous at first. The reason? Hormones.

Over the years, the balance of testosterone and oestrogen in the body changes. This can cause the tissue of the prostate to grow.

Imagine the small walnut mutating into a medium-sized peach - no joke. The problem? An enlarged prostate can press on the urethra and block the flow of urine. The result: you're constantly running to the loo, but you don't feel like you're "finished". Super annoying, isn't it?

When will it get serious?

Most men only experience the more harmless symptoms such as frequent urination, especially at night. But there are also risks: If the prostate becomes too large or is left untreated, it can lead to urinary tract infections or even kidney problems. And then, of course, there is prostate cancer to keep an eye on.

Prostate check: the brave win

A check-up with a urologist is not a test of courage. It's a preventive measure that could add years to your quality of life. If you're thinking: "Oh, that doesn't affect me", let me tell you - it affects us all. The good news is that a short appointment can bring clarity and clear your head.

What can you do yourself?

Here are a few basics on how you can do something good for your prostate:

1. **Healthy diet**: less fast food, more vegetables. Tomatoes, broccoli and walnuts in particular are prostate favourites.

2. **Exercise**: Sport not only helps your cardiovascular system, but also your prostate. So get off the sofa and get moving.

3. **Drink, but drink properly**: lots of water, less alcohol. Coffee in moderation. Your bladder and prostate will thank you.

4. **Regular check-ups**: Don't call your bluff. An annual check-up with a urologist from the age of 50 (or earlier if it runs in the family) is worth its weight in gold.

It's not a taboo, it's your life

The most important thing: stop suppressing the issue. It's not a sign of weakness to take care of your health - on the contrary. It shows that you are taking responsibility for yourself and the people who love you.

So, guys, enough with the excuses. Prostate check? Easy. Stay healthy? Even better. Anyone who finds this embarrassing hasn't heard the shot. Remember: a real man takes care of himself - before it's too late.

Sleep disorders and regeneration - why you should finally sleep again

You know how it is: you used to be able to sleep whenever and wherever you wanted. Put your head on the pillow, switch off the light and off you went. Now things are different. You lie awake, turn from side to side and your thoughts go round and round. In the morning, you feel like you've been run over by a truck. Welcome to the world of sleep disorders - a real highlight of the male menopause. But hey, don't panic, there are ways out of this dilemma.

Why do men sleep worse during the menopause?

The problem lies in your hormone balance, more precisely: in testosterone and melatonin.

- **Testosterone:** This miracle hormone, which makes us men strong, vital and self-confident, decreases during the menopause. Unfortunately, testosterone also plays a key role in regeneration and deep sleep. Less testosterone therefore means less restful sleep.

- **Melatonin:** This is your sleep hormone. It is released by the pineal gland in the evening and ensures that your body realises: "Time for rest." Melatonin production decreases with age - one reason why many men have problems falling asleep later in life.

But that's not all. Stress, worries and worries do the rest. Your family, your job, your health - all this can rob you of sleep at night. What's more, the menopause often brings with it increased sensitivity. Noises, light or even an uncomfortable mattress can suddenly have a disturbing effect.

The consequences of sleep deprivation

Poor sleep is not only annoying, it also has far-reaching consequences:

- **Mood swings and irritability:** lack of sleep makes you moody and thin-skinned. This can put a strain on your relationships.

- **Concentration problems:** People who sleep badly think more slowly and make more mistakes.

- **Weight gain:** Lack of sleep affects your hormonal balance and makes it harder to burn fat.

- **Health risks:** Long-term sleep deprivation increases the risk of cardiovascular disease, diabetes and a weakened immune system.

What is melatonin and why is it so important?

Melatonin is your natural sleep hormone. It is produced in the pineal gland when it gets dark and signals to your body that it's time to wind down. However, as you get older, your body produces less of it. The result: you fall asleep less easily and wake up more often.

The good news is that you can take melatonin as a dietary supplement. There are tablets, capsules or even sprays that can help restore your sleep rhythm. But beware: melatonin is not a miracle cure. It supports your body, but is only one building block. It is best to talk to your doctor beforehand to see if it is suitable for you.

Strategies for better sleep during the menopause

If you want to sleep like a baby again, try these tips:

1. **Create an ideal sleeping environment:** your bedroom should be dark, quiet and cool. Invest in good blackout curtains, a comfortable bed and - most importantly - an ergonomic pillow.

2. **Establish fixed rituals:** go to bed at the same time every night and get up at the same time in the morning. Routine is a real game changer for better sleep.

3. **Avoid screen time:** Smartphones, tablets and televisions emit blue light, which inhibits melatonin production. Switch them off at least one hour before going to bed.

4. **Pay attention to your diet:** lightly in the evening and avoid caffeine, sugar and alcohol. A calming tea, such as camomile or lavender, can work wonders.

5. **Reduce stress:** Meditation, yoga or simply taking a deep breath - there are many ways to clear your head. Write down your thoughts in the evening to get them out of your head.

6. **Food supplements:** In addition to melatonin, there is also magnesium, which relaxes your muscles and promotes sleep. Omega-3 fatty acids can also help to stabilise your hormone balance.

7. **Exercise:** Regular exercise improves the quality of sleep. But be careful: intensive training shortly before going to bed can have the opposite effect.

When should you see a doctor?

If none of this helps and you continue to have sleep problems, it may be time to see a doctor. There are many causes of sleep disorders that can be treated medically - from sleep apnoea to psychological stress. A sleep laboratory can provide clarity here.

Why sleep is so important

Sleep is not just rest time, but the phase in which your body regenerates. Your muscles grow, your brain sorts information and your immune system is strengthened. Without a good night's sleep, you are not only tired but also less efficient - and nobody wants that, right?

So, guys, take this topic seriously. A good night's sleep is not a minor matter, but the key to a fitter, happier and healthier life. Sleep well - for real!

Snoring - when the nights become a test of endurance

Snoring. An issue that is annoying for many men - and even more so for their partners. You may not even realise how loudly you snore while your other half is climbing the walls next to you. Snoring is not only annoying, it can also be a real test for your relationship. And: it's not just a "little night-time problem", but often an indication that something is wrong with your body.

It was also extreme for me. My wife had already put big pillows on her ears. When I snored so loudly that she couldn't stand it any longer, I had to "emigrate" to the guest room so that she could sleep peacefully and be fit for her job in elderly care.

In my case, the trigger was a completely deformed nasal septum. I had practised karate in my youth. I often got hit on the nose. I "treated" the many broken noses myself. Because you're a very tough person and don't go to the doctor. The end of the story: my nose was slightly crooked, but totally deformed on the inside.

At some point I went to the ENT doctor and had my airflow measured. Alarming: 0 per cent on the left, 11 per cent on the right. Of course, if you can't get air through your nose, you breathe through your mouth. This is very bad in many respects. For one thing, it's bad for your blood oxygen level - in my case it was far too low, at just 94 per cent. Secondly, it's also bad for sleeping through the night.

This caused even more problems: I was constantly sleep-deprived, bad-tempered and had blood pressure problems. My blood pressure was 155/120 at rest - simply far too high. Since then, I've also had to take antihypertensives. My belly grew and I put on a lot of weight. At 175 cm tall, I finally weighed 95 kilograms.

I hated the treadmill when I was exercising. After ten minutes I was already fed up. As a young man, I used to run around a lake with a mate every third day - 22.5 kilometres, which was easy back then. Now I was fed up after just 1.5 kilometres. Or not - because I couldn't get any air through my nose.

The doctor advised me to have a nasal septum operation to get the snoring under control. But in Berlin it was a real disaster to get an appointment for an operation. I then went to the Parkklinik in Wei-ßensee. I went for my first examination and they told me that they couldn't operate on me yet because I weighed too much. There could be problems with the anaesthetic.

I should lose ten kilos and then come back. Great - ten kilos! How is that supposed to work? But I managed it in two months by cutting out carbohydrates almost completely. I then reported back to the clinic and we arranged an appointment for an operation.

However, losing weight already had a positive effect: I snored a lot less and much more quietly. As a result, I was able to sleep with my wife again and she hardly ever banished me to the guest room. Which in turn was good for our togetherness.

Anyway, I then went to the operating theatre. I had the operation in May. The whole operation took four days. It was amazing that they did such a good job that I was again as soon as I came out of the operating theatre.able to breathe fully I felt extremely alert because my "noggin" was properly flooded with oxygen again.

I didn't even have a spectacle haematoma, just a plastic splint on my nose and a small tube to drain the blood. I also had **no pain** - not even at the surgical scar. I need **didn't any painkillers**. So I can only warmly recommend this clinic to anyone.

The wound - my nasal septum was completely rebuilt from my own cartilage tissue - healed after three weeks. Everything went really well. Even now, three years later, I can breathe through my nose again, I no longer snore and I am more efficient at sport again.

Alternative medical treatments

If the simple measures are not enough, you should consult a doctor. There are various medical approaches:

Sleep apnoea therapy: A CPAP mask can help with sleep apnoea. It ensures that the airways remain open by continuously supplying air pressure. **But let's be honest:** do you want to look like Darth Vader and lie next to your wife wearing one of these masks? I certainly don't. I was just too macho for that - it was never an option for me. When she wakes up at night and sees a cyborg like that lying next to her, she probably also thinks: "I wish I'd married the guy with the other moped that I didn't choose back then." Hahaha!

Dental splints/nose clips: These splints hold the lower jaw slightly forwards to keep the airways open. They are often a good solution for mild to moderate snoring. **Exactly the same rubbish:** it doesn't solve the underlying problem - namely the airflow and the excess weight. I also used nose clips all the time before the operation. If the septum is deformed, they don't help either. What are they supposed to widen? It doesn't work if the septum looks like a chequerboard.

So forget the nonsense and save your money. Surgery is the only effective method. Anyone who tells you otherwise is a charlatan or has no idea.

How snoring strains the relationship

Separate bedrooms: For many couples, snoring is the reason why they stop sleeping together at some point. This may help in the short term, but in the long run it often leads to alienation. The closeness that comes from falling asleep and waking up together is suddenly missing.

Poor sleep for your partner: snoring robs your partner of sleep. Constantly waking up because someone next to you is snoring like a jackhammer makes you tired and irritable. This irritability then manifests itself during the day - and conflicts are inevitable.

Feeling of ignorance: If the snorer does nothing about the problem, the partner often feels left alone. The impression is created: "He doesn't care about my peace and quiet."

Stress and emotional distance: The lack of sleep causes stress on both sides. The partner feels annoyed, the snorer may feel attacked or ashamed. This dynamic can damage the relationship.

Other possible causes for your snoring:

Overweight: Fat deposits in the throat can narrow the airways. A few extra kilos on the ribs therefore significantly increase the risk of snoring. This became more and more apparent to me the heavier I got.

Alcohol: Alcohol relaxes the muscles in the throat. This relaxation can cause the airways to collapse and increase snoring. I can only agree with this. Once we had a few cocktails in the evening on holiday, our night's sleep was over.

I shouted at the whole hotel so that other guests were already banging on the wall. Very embarrassing for my wife and me. Especially as I could only go into the bathroom because of the cramped conditions. I often slept in the bath or on the balcony if there was no bath.

But you're also disturbing the other guests. Once on holiday in Greece, I even went to the beach and slept on a sun lounger. Not a good idea on holiday in a foreign country. That could end badly. Fortunately, it didn't.

Sleeping position: Sleeping on your back favours snoring because the tongue falls backwards and blocks the airways.

Age: With age, the muscles in the throat lose their elasticity, which increases the risk of snoring.

Sex and passion - now let's get down to business

Sex has always been important to me, especially good sex. That's why I've never been to a prostitute in my entire life. I've also never been to a table dance bar, nor have I ever seen a porn film. It's always been unfathomable to me how you can buy a men's magazine, look at it, be totally hot and then not get rid of your energy. So it's rubbish.

I also never had one-night stands or sex with several women at the same time. Although I have to honestly admit that this was on my bucket list for a long time.

Good sex is now possible with love and a strong bond. That's my view. Other men don't have to share this view, but I think many see it the way I do.

Now let's talk straight guys. Sure, when we were 25 we could maintain an erection all night and never get enough.

For me, it was often the case that the women couldn't take any more at some point. At some point after five or six times a night, I had an extreme permanent erection. In my memories, that was always the best sex. Especially when my partner was doing really well and I brought her to climax several times. I was probably also genetically very lucky in the relationship as I always had a desire for women.

I like an offensive partner during sex who shows me what she wants but still gives me the power to do what I want with her. The best sex is when I notice how she slowly gets more and more off and I bring her to climax.

What does sex look like at 57? First of all: I hate scheduled sex. Nothing is worse for both parties than being told exactly when sex has to take place.

This is more for couples who don't really want to be with each other anymore, but where SHE doesn't want HIM to change his mind or vice versa. Here, sex is not there to build and deepen a bond, but only for the sake of "good peace".

Such couples do not talk about their sex or their desires and if they do, such an argument is accompanied by mutual accusations and recriminations.

My wife and I once overheard such a conversation live. We were invited to a garden party at a friend's house when a couple started arguing. We didn't realise what it was actually about until the two of them started shouting at each other. Let's call them Katja and Thomas.

Katja accused Thomas of always coming too quickly and Thomas accused Katja of not having sex for a year and that Katja always lies there like a board during sex and doesn't even taken from behind- want to be . Hahaha really funny to say something like that in front of the whole team.

My God, I felt sorry for Thomas, it's clear that he comes quickly when he hasn't had sex for a year. "She's crazy, that trulla" I thought to myself.

Not letting the man have his way for a year but then getting upset that he comes too quickly. It's like someone dealing you a pack of cards in a poker game and then demanding that you win. That doesn't work.

Thomas also looks really good, very sporty, tall, well-groomed blond guy.

Katja: she looks like she's pulling "catapults to Gondor" after work, small, chubby, short red hair, big arms and bum, zero charisma.

Katja had obviously "given up" after her first and only child, under the motto, "I'm a mum now, it's all about the child".

I said quietly to myself: "Old lady, look in the mirror, be glad that someone wants to fuck you at all".

My wife looked at me in horror, pinched my arm and said: "Shut up, not so loud. Are you daft? You can't say things like that".

Our friends, Nadine and Uwe, were standing next to us. They over-heard my comment and just grinned, I had probably hit the nail on the head with my spiteful comment.

The argument between Katja and Thomas culminated in Katja slapping Thomas in the face. That was the highlight of the party.

Because of the bad vibes, we were no longer in the mood for the party and went with Nadine and Uwe to our favourite ouzologist (Greek).

About a year later, we heard from acquaintances that Katja and Thomas had split up. He had probably "procured" another partner immediately after the argument.

It reminded me of the incident with my first wife and the subsequent cheating. I just thought to myself: "That old woman is so crazy, she deserves it, how can a woman treat her husband so badly". It's just a shame for the child, who is now growing up without a father.

As I said, back to the subject of SPEAKING. Why don't you guys just tell each other what you like and what you want? How is your partner supposed to guess what's going on in your head? You know: no arms, no biscuits. So be brave and say "I want to..." You can't get more than a "no".

Topic: (S)experiments

Personally, I think that you should communicate openly what you want from your partner - especially in bed. **How is she supposed to guess what you want, guys, if you don't say it clearly?** That's exactly what I agreed with my wife. There are no taboos with us, at least when it comes to talking. We talk openly about everything we like and what's important to us. The only things we've ticked off are partner-swapping and swinger parties. **That's a no-go for both of us and will never be on the table.** We both agree on that.

Swapping partners? Absolutely out of the question for me. I just don't think I could bear to see another man with my wife. The thought alone is enough to make me draw a red line. **How am I supposed to cope if I have to watch another bloke being inside my wife?** No thanks, I'm out of there. What I could imagine, though, would be watching other couples having sex - but without getting active my-self. Somehow the idea of seeing others letting themselves go without being involved ourselves appeals to me. **That's perhaps a line I could draw.**

What I've noticed in recent years is that many men think that their wives lose interest in sex after the menopause. Sure, that can happen. **But I can tell you that sex with a woman my age is often even more sensual and relaxed than before.** Without that annoying pressure to perform, without unrealistic expectations. It's no longer about delivering some kind of "performance", but simply about enjoying the time together. Sex may be slower, quieter, but it is often much more intense. It's a whole new level of intimacy. But for this, you guys need to know what happens to your wife during the menopause - physically and emotionally.

As far as I'm concerned, I still love having sex with my wife. And one reason for this is certainly that she still looks fantastic at the age of 55. **Long legs, a great bust - and her blonde curls, which are all tousled in the morning, make me weak every time.** I affectionately call her my "surfer chick" or "Private Pam", a reference to the old Pamela Anderson from "Baywatch". Our sex is often spontaneous, nothing exciting in the sense of wild experiments, but incredibly sensual. Sometimes it doesn't take much more than a glance from her and it's already sizzling.

I will probably never forget one experience. I came home from one of my photo tours. Camera in hand, sweaty, tired, ready for the couch. But there she was - my wife, relaxed, a mischievous grin on her face. She looked at me and said: **"Say, can't you take a few nice pictures of me?"** I thought it was just something I'd said, so I jokingly replied: **"Sure, sweetheart, but then take your clothes off!"** I had no idea what I had set in motion.

She disappeared into her dressing room without a word and came out a few minutes later. **And I swear to you, I couldn't believe my eyes.** She had thrown on a pair of red overknees and a see-through, red romper and I was blown away. Until that moment, I didn't realise what a damn sexy woman I had at home. So I grabbed the camera and started photographing her in all kinds of poses. It got hot - really hot. And every time I tried to touch her, she pushed my hand away and slapped my fingers.

143

But at some point, she could no longer resist, and neither could I. **And what happened next? Well, I literally fell over her.**

It was one of those moments that burns itself deep into your memory because it was so full of passion and fun at the same time. These are the moments when you realise that sex doesn't have to be boring in a long-term relationship - on the contrary.

It can even get better because you know each other better and know how to make the other person happy.

So, guys, be honest. Tell your wife what you want, what you need and what is important to you. Don't wait for her to read your thoughts. **Communication is the key - not only in everyday life, but especially in bed.** This is the only way you can really get the best out of your relationship and maybe even experience a few surprises that you never expected.

Menopause in women: Effects, symptoms and changes in sexual behaviour

The menopause, also known as the menopause, is a natural phase in a woman's life that marks the end of her fertile years. This transition, which typically occurs between the ages of 45 and 55, is accompanied by a variety of physical and emotional changes. This article describes in detail the effects and symptoms of the menopause, the changes in sexual behaviour and possible measures to alleviate symptoms.

Causes and phases of the menopause

The menopause is characterised by a natural decline in the production of the female sex hormones oestrogen and progesterone. This process takes place in several phases:

Premenopause: The years before the actual onset of the menopause, when hormone production is already beginning to fluctuate.

Perimenopause: This phase covers the time immediately before the menopause and can last several years. The menstrual cycles become more irregular.

Menopause: The time when a woman has not had a period for twelve months.

Postmenopause: The years after the menopause, during which the symptoms can gradually subside.

Symptoms of the menopause

The symptoms of the menopause can be diverse and vary from person to person. The most common include

Hot flushes and night sweats: Sudden sensations of heat, often accompanied by sweating.

Sleep disorders: Problems falling asleep and staying asleep, often caused by night sweats.

Mood swings: Increased irritability, anxiety and depression.

Weight gain: Changes in metabolism can lead to an increase in body weight.

Cognitive changes: Concentration problems and memory disorders.

Vaginal dryness and atrophy: Reduced moisture and elasticity of the vaginal mucosa, which can lead to discomfort and pain during sexual intercourse.

Decreased libido: A decrease in sexual desire.

Changes in sexual behaviour

During the menopause, women can experience various changes in their sexual behaviour and sexual health:

Vaginal dryness: This can make sexual intercourse painful and impair sexual activity. Using lubricants and vaginal moisturisers can help.

Decreased libido: Hormonal changes can lead to a decrease in sexual desire. Communication with your partner and an open approach to your own needs and concerns are important.

Psychological influences: Mood swings and depressive moods can affect sexual desire. Psychological support or couples therapy can be helpful.

Measures to alleviate the symptoms

There are various approaches to alleviating the symptoms of the menopause and improving quality of life:

Hormone replacement therapy (HRT): Taking oestrogen and progesterone can alleviate many symptoms of the menopause. However, this therapy should be individualised and carried out under medical supervision, as it can be associated with risks.

Phytoestrogens: Natural oestrogens from plants, which are contained in soya, linseed and certain food supplements, can help to balance hormonal fluctuations.

Lifestyle changes: A healthy diet, regular exercise and stress management techniques can help control symptoms. Weight training and cardiovascular exercise in particular can have a positive effect on health.

Sleep hygiene: Measures to improve sleep, such as creating a quiet sleeping environment and avoiding caffeine and alcohol before bedtime, can counteract sleep disorders.

Psychological support: Counselling or therapy can help to deal with the emotional changes. Group or individual therapies offer support and coping strategies.

Vaginal treatments: Local oestrogen treatments in the form of creams, tablets or rings can relieve vaginal dryness and atrophy.

Lubricants and moisturisers.: The use of water- or silicone-based lubricants can reduce sexual discomfort and make sexual intercourse more enjoyable

Conclusion

The menopause is a natural phase of life that every woman goes through. Although it can be associated with a range of unpleasant symptoms, there are many ways to alleviate them and improve well-being. A combination of medical treatments, lifestyle changes and psychological support can help women manage this transitional period in a positive and healthy way. Open dialogue with doctors, partners and friends is crucial.

Accept getting old - or when it's not just memories that become a nuisance

The central issue that concerns me is getting old. Somehow I have the feeling that time is running faster and faster. I've only just celebrated New Year's Eve and the next one is just around the corner. Caught up in the daily grind, the days, weeks and months fly by. And yet another year of life has passed, and the years that lie ahead are becoming fewer and fewer.

Another thing that concerns me is the number of mates my age who die suddenly and unexpectedly. Sure, Covid has taken a few. But there were also mates who were perfectly fit and died suddenly. One example is a friend from airsoft. Airsoft is a military strategy game, basically like "Call of Duty", only in real life.

We dress up like real SEALs and chase each other through the forest on old Russian military bases. To do this, we use air rifles from which small plastic bullets are fired. The rifles have a range of around 50 metres. The impact energy is harmless and acts like a bee sting. An opponent who is hit shouts "hit" and leaves the playing field.

He goes to a spawn point and can immediately start the game again from there. There are missions and mission scenarios. Due to the short combat distances, the game comes very close to real mission scenarios, especially in building combat at short distances, in dark, half-ruined buildings - a really creepy feeling.

For example, our team was trained by someone who had been a Bundeswehr instructor in Afghanistan for eight years. He taught us a lot, including tactics in building combat and in the field. He always said that it was very similar to the real madness, except that we weren't in mortal danger and there were no grenades or mortars.

The game is fun and appeals to the male hunting instinct. For example, I still have a lot of adrenalin in me two days after a game and feel intoxicated. I could always go back to immediately and keep playing. The game is addictive - I know people who play every weekend.

The great thing is that the airsoft guns are modelled deceptively similar to real weapons. For example, I have airsoft markers modelled on an M249 machine gun, a World War II Tommy gun, a BAR 1918, an M1 Garand and an SVD Dragunov Sniper Rifle, and many more.

As the weights of the markers, the loading process, the functions and the magazines are also modelled on the original, this creates an extremely authentic atmosphere. The markers often also work using the blowback method: Here, part of the air pressure energy is used to open the breech and move the bolt back and forth.

This produces a metallic-sounding noise and a recoil that is comparable to that of an original AR15 or M4, for example. Everything feels very realistic. What's more, the enemy also tries to get you, so you have to be tactical and set traps for your opponents.

We visit these old military bases once or twice a month. Around Berlin, there were Russian positions about six kilometres apart, such as barracks, rocket positions, tank battalions, artillery, command posts, bunkers, radar stations and air bases.

That's why these lost places are usually located deep in the forest. They often look like you've landed in Chernobyl's abandoned city of Pripyat.

Examples include the old poison gas factory in Briesen, the Harnekop nuclear bunker and the SA-2 missile base in Prötzel. These sites mostly consist of bunkers, old production halls, blocks of flats and barracks.

These buildings consist of many rooms that are morbid, run-down and abandoned. This charm of decay alone gives a very queasy and eerie feeling. Basements in these buildings are usually pitch dark and flooded. You have to wade through deep water with a lamp on your helmet. The feeling is indescribable.

As we also have a WW2 re-enactment project going on, which is modelled on the "Band of Brothers" series, the atmosphere is heightened even further. We wear uniforms and equipment from the period, for example the 101st Airborne Paratrooper. We also only use markers that are modelled on weapons from that era, such as the Tommy Gun, Kar98, PPSh, BAR, M1 Garand, Arisaka and so on. The Americans only speak English on the field, there is no radio, only field telephones from the Second World War. We then re-enact battles from the Second World War. Simply great cinema.

Me the "Lone Survivor "

My friend was a fit, well-trained guy, 52 years old. We stormed up the sand hill in Harnekop and cleared the enemy positions at breakneck speed with 20 kilos of kit. I was always amazed at how fit he still was for his age, which of course also applied to me.

He died suddenly while digging a ditch on his property. Without any previous illnesses, just like that. It was a real shock and kept me very busy for many months. I now saw directly and brutally how quickly the light can be switched off. As a result, my "neighbourhood" became increasingly thin, and good friends and comrades were gone forever.

All that remains is melancholy and the memories of a great time with great people. Time passes incessantly, the years fade away. That's what really bothers me. At least that's how I feel. The years that still lie ahead of me are definitely not many.

I missed my "wingman" at every game and often think about how often he "covered my fire" and what great moves we pulled off together.

Once we cleared an entire building of 25 enemies in pairs, without support, and were the heroes of the day. Another time, we set up a sniper position together on an old airport tower and hit 15 enemies. He was my spotter/supporter and I was the shooter. The action reminded me a lot of the film "American Sniper".

I'm often overcome with sadness on the pitch when I come to places where we had great experiences.

So he remains unforgotten for me and is somehow still there. I ask myself whether anyone will remember me once I'm gone.

I often ask myself this question when I go to sleep at night. Will I wake up again? You can often see in the news recently how quickly life can come to an end. Violence, war and natural disasters are increasing dramatically.

Perhaps at our age we shouldn't plan so far into the future, but live more in the here and now and savour the moments we experience?

Class reunion after 30 years - Holy shit, we're old

The class reunion two years ago was like a heavy slap in the face - our first reunion after a good 30 years, and as soon as I entered the room, I felt like I was in a time machine that had left a bitter aftertaste. Of the ten boys in our class, only three were still alive. Seven had already passed away, and that was a real shock. Most of them had lost their battle with cancer, and at the age of just 45 to 50. Life can be merciless, I thought to myself.

I hardly recognised any of the girls. I hadn't seen them since school and somehow I had imagined that perhaps very little had changed. But reality quickly caught up with me. Almost all of them had put on a lot of weight and looked like they had brought half the buffet with them. Even my first secret crush, the most beautiful girl in the class, was barely recognisable. Formerly with long, shiny hair and bright eyes, she had now become an unsightly older lady with a mop of purple hair and thick glasses that covered half her face. The feeling of youth that she once awakened in me was blown away.

It was a bittersweet experience, the class reunion. We swapped stories, laughed about old pranks and reminisced about our fights and romances. But somewhere there was always the nagging feeling of how much time had passed and how fleeting life is.

Some had raised their children, others were married for the second time, others talked about their hobbies that helped them to enjoy the "quieter" phase of life. The conversations were characterised by a touch of nostalgia, but also the realisation that we have all grown older - and that time is catching up with us bit by bit.

How should you deal with it? In any case, I told myself that I should enjoy life. I now try to let beautiful things affect me more and enjoy them. I always tell myself now: who knows how long and how often you can still experience something like this?

Especially when it comes to activities with my friends, I now ask myself more and more often how often we will see each other again.

Even when I'm travelling with my wife, we have a good time and don't let ourselves get stressed anymore. If people get on our nerves, we disappear and go somewhere else.

I no longer feel like getting annoyed by ignorant, ill-mannered and cheeky pissants. We've been doing quite well with that recently. Or we look for locations that are eco- and child-free. "Adults only" is the new magic word.

We already have six grandchildren and I can't stand the shouting any more. I'm actually happy when they leave again after three to four hours. Sounds crass, but it's the truth. In moments like these, I always realise that a younger partner with a desire to have children would never have made me happy. The sex couldn't have been so good that I would do that to myself again.

Physically, I don't notice my ageing that much yet. In any case, I still feel fit enough. Sure, I'm no longer running marathons and I'm struggling to get rid of my belly, but overall I'm doing well.

This experience really made me realise how quickly everything can change. Last year, I almost lost my life because of a small but highly dangerous virus that completely threw my body off track.

It started with a gastrointestinal illness that quickly worsened and ultimately even led to kidney failure. If my doctor and my wife hadn't been so insistent that I go to hospital, I probably wouldn't still be here today.

A short hospitalisation, several tests and infusions later, I was fortunately back on my feet. This experience made me realise that a small virus can become a danger faster than you think and suddenly you're on the edge of your seat.

Since then, I've been taking better care of myself and taking my check-ups more seriously. We are very lucky to live in Germany, where medical check-ups are well organised - and almost free of charge. It's annoying and takes time, but I'd rather invest a few hours than pay the price for my negligence at some point.

That's just part of getting older - and also the fact that the grandchildren now cheerfully call you "Grandad". Sure, I'm still out and about in stylish, ripped jeans and modern outfits, and I make sure I stay fit. But that doesn't change the fact that 60 is just around the corner.

When I think back to my own grandparents or what other men looked like when they were 60, the difference is huge. In the past, 60-year-olds often looked like ancient grandpas with hats, stiff suits and a halting gait. Today, on the other hand, I feel and look more like a sporty, active man. And that's exactly how I want it to stay! I'm determined to do everything I can to preserve this attitude to life and not just get "older", but to go my own way.

The spirituality of men - faith, the search for meaning and the big questions of life

I was never a religious person. Faith and spirituality didn't play a big role in my life for a long time. For me, everyday life was determined by tangible realities - work, family, goals that I set myself and wanted to achieve. But as life goes on, there are these moments that touch you in a way you didn't expect and they force you to stop and reflect.

One of these moments happened on a trip to Greece, on the island of Rhodes. It was an experience that I still can't fully explain, but it changed something in me.

One day we visited Butterfly Valley, a magical place full of life and dotted with mystical-looking trees and small waterfalls. It looked like a fairytale forest, almost like the Elven Forest from **Lord of the Rings**. The air was filled with the sounds of nature, the rustling of the leaves, the rippling of the water, and you could literally feel that this place had a special energy. As a hobby photographer, I discovered countless motifs that intensified my enthusiasm for this place. Every tree, every clearing offered something new, something magical.

At the end of the climb through the valley, we came to a small monastery that was hidden away on a hill, as if it had been there for centuries. A few other visitors were also there, but the atmosphere was quiet, almost reverent. In front of the monastery stood an old monk selling rosaries, holy water and necklaces with wooden crosses at a small stall. He had a long grey beard, wore a worn brown monk's habit and looked like Father Christmas - with a big belly and incredibly loving eyes. It was as if this man came from another time, as if he carried a wisdom that went beyond the everyday.

I was struck by the beauty of the valley and the peaceful atmosphere of the monastery. Suddenly I noticed the monk looking over at me. He came over from his little stall and walked straight towards me. Without saying a word, he took one of the chains with a wooden cross, hung it around my neck and hugged me. He said something in Greek that I didn't understand, but it didn't matter. At that moment, something happened that I still can't really put into words. I suddenly started crying. I don't know why, but it was as if a burden was lifted from me that I hadn't even realised I was carrying until then. It was as if this man - this stranger - had taken away everything that was weighing me down without me ever telling him. I felt loved and accepted in a way I hadn't expected.

He continued to hold me while I cried, and the mood around us seemed to change. The other visitors, who had previously been quietly exploring the monastery, were suddenly moved too. Some women also began to cry, as if my emotions had triggered something in them. It was a moment of deep connection that I had never experienced before. Everything around me seemed to stand still, as if the world had stopped for a moment.

My wife came to me a few minutes later after buying some water from a kiosk. She could hardly believe what she was seeing. In all the years of our marriage, she had never seen me cry, and now I was standing there, held by a strange monk, my eyes full of tears. It was a moment that touched us both deeply. She knew immediately that something had broken open inside me, something that had been hidden for a long time. After the monk finally let go of me, we went into the monastery's small chapel together to enjoy the silence. It was as if this silence was exactly what I needed after the emotional storm.

That day, that moment, changed something in me. It was one of the key experiences in my life so far, a turning point that made me think about the meaning of life. I had never really thought about the deeper meaning of my existence before, but that moment in Butterfly Valley stayed with me. From then on, I began to think more about the big questions of life. What is the meaning of our existence? Why are we here? What comes after death?

I wouldn't say that I've become religious since this experience. It's not that I suddenly believe in a particular deity or religion. But I have started to look for answers - not necessarily in a spiritual or religious context, but within myself. I realised that there is more to life than just everyday life and the goals we set ourselves. There are those moments when life forces us to pause and reflect, and I believe that Butterfly Valley was such a moment for me.

Since then, I have been looking more closely at the big questions in life, not necessarily in the hope of finding all the answers, but in order to understand myself better. This moment showed me that sometimes there are things that we 't explaincan but that still touch us deeply. It was as if this monk had struck a chord in me that I hadn't heard before. A string that searches for meaning, for connection and for inner peace.

Perhaps that is the true meaning of spirituality: the ability to pause in moments of stillness and the beauty of life and realise that we are all part of something bigger. Whether that is a divine plan or simply the beauty of nature that surrounds us is ultimately irrelevant. What matters is that we open ourselves up to these moments and are willing to let go of the burdens we unconsciously carry around with us.

This moment in Butterfly Valley showed me that it is never too late to search for meaning - and that this search, no matter where it leads, can be an enrichment for your own life.

The second formative event in my life was our visit to the Hagia Sophia during a city trip to Istanbul. This place simply overwhelmed me. **The atmosphere there is full of power and history, the magic of this place is almost tangible.** You can feel how important it is for the people and the culture. The walls tell of centuries of intersecting faith, power and history - a place that radiates the depth of human spirituality and devotion. It's hard to describe, but there in that gigantic dome, surrounded by all that history and meaning, I suddenly realised what an incredible woman I have by my side.

At that moment, I decided to spontaneously propose to my wife in front of everyone. It just felt right. Right because she had forgiven me so much, because she is the greatest and most loving person I know. The woman who has stood by me through all my escapades, who has never turned her back on me - **the most loyal partner imaginable.** So what better place to renew our vows and make a fresh start? It was there, in this atmosphere, that I decided to take the opportunity to and leave everything behind to start a new chapter with a second wedding.

The moment was full of emotion. Kneeling in front of all these people, in this powerful spiritual place that holds so much history, and telling my wife: **"I want to spend the rest of my life with you, no matter what has been, no matter what is to come."** That was one of the most honest moments of my life. I wanted to renew our love, leave everything negative, everything that had weighed us down, behind us and start again.

And what followed was one of the most beautiful days of our lives: **A year later, we got married again on the beach in Turkey.** The sun, the sea, the sand under our feet - it was perfect. A symbolic new beginning that I would never have thought possible long before. If I'm honest, I was a fool for forgetting how incredibly amazing my wife is. This second wedding was like an awakening for me. It was the moment when I realised that I had taken the happiness I have with her for granted far too often.

Sometimes we men have to go through crises to understand what really matters. **I had taken my wife for granted and forgotten how strong, how loving and how loyal she is.** This second wedding was not only a promise to her, but also to myself - to never again forget what a wonderful person I have by my side. It was a kind of spiritual renewal process. A deep sense of gratitude and humility flowed through me that day.

These moments of spirituality, whether in Hagia Sophia or on the beach at our second wedding, have shown me that there is more to life than just everyday life. It's not just about careers, problems or goals. It's about the people who are with us. It's about the love that sustains us. And it's about recognising the miracle of life that unfolds in moments like these.

This spiritual experience changed me. It helped me to see again what is really important. **Sometimes you need this deep, almost magical experience to step out of the fog of everyday life and reflect on what really nourishes your heart.** For me, it was my wife who was always there for me, even in moments when I didn't deserve it.

The spirituality I felt in these moments was not a religious revelation, but a deep awareness of what love and partnership really mean. **It's about commitment, forgiveness, loyalty and the ability to start again.** This second wedding was the symbolic act with which I proved to my wife, but also to myself, that we are worth fighting for our love and that it is never too late to make a new decision - for the person you love.

From that moment on, I vowed never to take my wife for granted again. **She is not only the woman who accompanies me on my journey through life, but also the one who shows me again and again what love really means.** And that is a realisation that I never want to let go of.

Does life have a meaning - or is everything already written?

Everyone has probably asked themselves the question of whether there is life after death. Religions say yes. In my opinion, however, religions are just an instrument of the powerful to control us anyway. Their concepts seem nonsense to me, especially the idea of a so-called life after death. I don't want to offend anyone - everyone should believe in what brings them fulfilment and comfort. Those who find peace in religion should be happy with it.

However, I maintain that there is no "Almighty Being", and I further maintain that there is not even free will. In my opinion, free will is an illusion and everything is predetermined. Why?

Determinism

Determinism is a hypothesis according to which every elementary particle has a predetermined path. We agree that all matter in the universe originated from a single point, a singularity, in the Big Bang. All elementary particles, i.e. the building blocks of all things, were created at this point. We also know that everything is based on physical laws, as we learnt at school. This also applies to the movement of every single elementary particle. We, our environment, everything that surrounds us is made up of elementary particles. The atoms of our body were formed in the core of a dying sun. We are literally stardust.

Let us imagine the path of a single particle since the Big Bang. The particle is attracted or repelled by other particles and has travelled a path since the Big Bang that is governed by the laws of physics.

Let's assume we had a supercomputer with unlimited computing power. This supercomputer could calculate the path of all particles in the universe. The computer knows the current location of every particle and could trace the path of every particle back to its origin, the Big Bang.

Do you recognise something? Exactly. If the computer can recalculate the path of the particles, it can also calculate the future path of each particle.

What does that mean? It means that the path of every particle is predetermined - from the Big Bang to the distant future. This means that free will is just an illusion. Because we, our thoughts and feelings, our environment - everything is made up of elementary particles and vibrations. Sounds esoteric? But it's not, it's logic.

When I first heard about this theory, I thought to myself: somehow it makes sense. A life full of decisions that we believe we can control - but in reality everything seems to follow a predetermined pattern. For me, there was only one conclusion: everything is predetermined and unchangeable. It was a liberating thought. Because if everything is predetermined and free will is just an illusion, then we are not to blame for what happens. We are no longer spectators in a play that has long since been written.

That may sound sobering at first, but I see it more as an invitation to become more relaxed. Why get upset about every little thing, why make an effort to force a certain path? If everything takes its course, why not sit back and take life as it is? Of course, this doesn't mean that we should give up or stop doing anything. But if you see life as a predetermined river that you can't swim against anyway, then a whole new sense of freedom opens up. It's not necessary to hold everything frantically in your hands.

Whether I am right in my assumption is up to you. You are like an engine driver travelling on rails in a train without a windscreen. You can only look out to the side. The route is given, but you don't see it as a whole, only where you are at that moment.

These facts will certainly come as a shock to some, because much of what they have learnt in the course of their lives contradicts my statement. But from the atoms that are released when our bodies decompose after death, something new is created again. The released atoms form new bonds and continue to do so until the end of time.

So, in a sense, religions are partly right: nothing is wasted; everything is recycled, and we become something else again. In this sense, the concept of reincarnation is even partly correct, at least in a certain respect.

Our consciousness, on the other hand, is a pure illusion that disappears when we die and is lost in every respect. This is because our thoughts and therefore our consciousness are the result of a complex biochemical process.

Of course, the major religions and those who hold the levers of power don't like the fact that we think about such things. The idea that everything could be predetermined, that our supposed free will is just an illusion - they don't want us to believe that. Why? Quite simply, once we allow the hypothesis of determinism to sink in, once we really realise what it means, we lose the urge to keep on functioning. We then no longer blindly submit to the expectations and ideas that the "powers that be" have mapped out for us.

Imagine what will happen when people stop playing this game. When we are no longer just working, paying taxes and consuming as cogs in an endless wheel so that a few at the top of the food chain can continue to live in prosperity and luxury. Because that's the trick, isn't it? They want to keep us busy - at work, consuming, in the eternal hunt for more. But it's an illusion that is only meant to tempt us to toil until the end of our lives while others profit from our labour.

Too pessimistic? Perhaps. But that's exactly why I say: think hard about it. We are not here to just end up as workers and consumers.

I will become the North Pole of my family

The wisdom of old age. That's the image I have in mind when I see a white-haired old man. However, wisdom doesn't necessarily apply to me after all these years and all the chaos I've caused. However, due to the many experiences and the constant falling down and getting up again, I can draw on a wealth of experience. This means I can be a good counsellor to my children and show them how not to do it.

However, it's often a shame that the children don't listen to you and inevitably have to go through the same experiences. In retrospect, they always say: "Dad, I wish I'd listened to you."

But let's be honest: did we listen to our parents? No, we also did our own thing. Looking back, I would have been spared a lot of suffering if I had listened to my parents straight away.

A good example of this is that my parents advised me against marrying my first wife. They had already realised what calibre she was. But I was blind and didn't recognise that. I have already described what happened in the previous chapter.

Basically, I "ruined" my whole life with this woman and the subsequent break-up. Who knows where I would be today and how many of my dreams I could have realised if I hadn't ended up with this woman. My dream was always to stop working at 50, live on a finca in Greece, look out to sea and enjoy the breeze.

Unfortunately, there is no reset button in life, you have to live with your wrong decisions and come to terms with them. I would sacrifice years of my life to start again and undo the mistakes.

The only thing I don't regret are the wonderful children I have. But back to the children and the role of the good counsellor. What I always admired about my late stepfather was that he was like a magnet that held the family together.

How did he manage that? Quite simply, he was always a good listener and counsellor. He patiently listened to every sh... and gave advice on how he would decide and why. Another important point was how he dealt with arguments. He hated arguments in the family and didn't allow them. He nipped arguments in the bud immediately by forcing the family members to find a solution and get along.

For him, family gatherings were an expression of loyalty. Anyone who didn't turn up was bombarded with phone calls until they did turn up.

The only time he allowed us not to turn up was on Boxing Day 2002, when it was minus 20 degrees, snowing and black ice on the roads. It was too dangerous for me to drive 60 kilometres on the motorway with my two small children and my wife. He realised it and said: "Boy, you're right, I could have thought of that myself." Two hours later, he was standing outside our house with his mother-in-law and a delicious roast goose. I was delighted and we had a really nice Boxing Day.

I thought that was great. I wanted to be like that when I was his age. Now I'm his age and I do it just like him. And lo and behold, it works.

I'm like a herding dog that protects its flock. I used to be a wolf who destroyed everything and did his own thing. Today, I see it as my job to keep my family together and protect them, just like my stepfather did. It's a role that means a lot to me and shows me that true strength doesn't lie in going through life alone, but in being there for the people you love.

Men's self-worth - career, family and the fear of failure

The menopause is not just a phase of physical change. It also causes men to pause and look back - at what they have achieved, at what they lack and at what still lies ahead. It's like looking in a mirror that shows not only your own image, but also all the expectations you have of yourself. And this look often brings to light insecurities that have long lain dormant.

A man's self-worth is put to the test during this phase in particular. For years, success, performance and recognition have defined a man - above all through his career. Your career was the pillar on which your self-confidence rested. You worked hard, perhaps with the aim of eventually feeling that you had arrived. But what happens when you realise that your professional success is not what you had hoped for? Or when your career path suddenly comes to a stand-still?

Something happens during the menopause that you don't expect: Your own worth is scrutinised. The question arises: **What have I achieved?** The answer is often sobering. The thought that it wasn't enough settles in. Perhaps there is that younger colleague who is rising with fresh energy, while you yourself have the feeling that you are treading water. You realise that professional fame may no longer shine as brightly as it used to. Suddenly your own importance in your professional environment seems less certain. Your once secure status begins to waver.

However, it is not only the career that is the focus of this critical self-reflection. The family role is also being re-examined. Many men have borne responsibility for their families for years, defining themselves as providers and protectors. But what happens when the children grow up and leave home? When the dynamics in the family change and the role of the father is suddenly less clear?

It's as if the foundation on which life was built is slowly cracking. **Who am I when my children no longer need me the way they used to?** This question accompanies many men in this phase of life, and it is not so easy to answer. In a society that often defines men by their role as breadwinners and protectors, this phase becomes a challenge. Their own identity is called into question.

Added to this is the fear of failure. This fear accompanies many men throughout their lives, but it becomes particularly pressing during the menopause. It is not just a question of whether you have achieved enough in the past, but also whether you are still relevant for the future. The thought that your best years may be behind you is hard to bear. **What if I haven't realised my potential? What if what comes next is just a descent?**

This fear can have a paralysing effect. It often leads to an attempt to go all out once again - be it through excessive professional ambition or the urge to prove oneself in other ways. Some men throw themselves into affairs or risky adventures because they feel they have to "live" one more time before it's too late. It is an attempt to prove to themselves that they are still in control.

But the truth is: This phase of life is not about proving something to yourself. It's about redefining your own self-worth. Because a man's value does not lie in his career or in the expectations that others have of him. It is about finding a new benchmark - one that is not based on external successes, but on inner strength and satisfaction.

The path to this realisation is not easy. It requires recognising your own insecurities and having the courage to let go of old ideas. It means not seeing the menopause as a threat, but as an opportunity to reinvent yourself. It's not about denying the past, but embracing it - with all its successes and failures. Because in the end, what counts is not what you have achieved, but how you see yourself.

This phase offers the opportunity to reflect on what really counts. Not the position in the job, not material success, but the question: **Who am I as a person**? By focusing on yourself and learning to recognise your own value apart from external validation, you can find the peace that you may have been looking for on the outside for years.

And as you redefine yourself, you can also learn to let go of the fear of failure. Because life is not a competition, and a man's value lies not in what he achieves, but in who he is. The menopause is not the end, but the beginning of a new chapter - a chapter in which self-worth no longer depends on external successes, but on inner strength and acceptance.

My bucket list - missed dreams, or not?

Our goals and life plans shape our lives, as do our dreams and ideas of what we want to achieve in life. But caught up in everyday problems and the daily grind, our dreams fade more and more until they are just a faint echo from the past or dissolve completely.

I can't stand all these supposed coaches who make us believe how great their lives are with a lifestyle financed on credit.

The truth is often far from it. The vast majority of people lead exactly the life I have described: It consists of work, obligations and the daily struggle, interrupted by a few beautiful moments.

You are enslaved by your everyday life and the compulsion to earn money in order to be able to live reasonably well at all.

For me, life has somehow lost its colour, the goals have disappeared and what remains is the bland aftertaste of resignation. Our world is run by unscrupulous psychopaths, by those who are only after power and profit and have no regard for losses.

Bit by bit they are driving us all towards the abyss, and as if that wasn't enough, we also have the politicians who complete the chaos, make life more and more difficult and only harass us further.

When I the faces of see on the election posters, I am gripped by an aversion that I can hardly put into words. I wish I could them all these figures stop seeing or wish I could press a big reset button.

My bucket list has never been long; I don't need nonsense like skydiving or bungee jumping to be happy.

My bucket list consisted of travelling and a good life. I always wanted to stop working at 50 and live somewhere in Spain or Greece in the sun - a house by the sea and a simple life.

I almost made it with some of my business ideas, but some crap happened in the world that threw a spanner in the works.

If your dreams are shattered, it is NOT YOUR FAULT. I dare say that this diabolical world even actively ensures that YOU CANNOT realise ANY OF YOUR DREAMS.

You should remain cheap consumer and labour cattle, trapped and bound to your "floe". Best of all...

...heavily in debt for stuff you don't need,

...with a house that you'll have to pay off by the time you retire and will probably lose when pissants like the Greens up with a come that forces you into new debts,heating law

...with a fancy car bought on credit so that you can shine with your neighbours, who you probably think are shit anyway,

...with a pet that makes sure you don't move away from your "clod" and every holiday starts with putting the animal somewhere,

...and with the latest tech nonsense so they can monitor you 24/7 and track everything you do - when, where and with whom you talk and know all your secrets!

The funny thing is that you haven't even realised what a bizarre, shitty and permanent enslavement you live in!

To top it off, they always show you the "rich and beautiful" on television and tell you that you can have that too.

What diabolical, abysmally evil sarcasm orchestrated by some narcissistic psychopaths.

The truth is: these "great beautiful people" were either born with the "golden spoon" in their mouths or they were artificially "pushed" just to show you what a pathetic little sausage you are.

I'm sure they'll get a kick out of the thought and laugh their heads off at us lemmings.

Look at guys like the owners of Amazon or Tesla, they openly laugh at you and say to your face: "Go and fuck yourself."

These anti-social scumbags - let's call them billionaire parasites - want you to plough even more to get to the supposed upper class.

But they certainly don't want you to feel any better, and you will never manage it for the reasons mentioned. You live in a deceptive illusory world. Just like the biggest liar, deceiver and cheat of all time wants: the devil!

But the joke is that you will never achieve this lifestyle. Speculators, politicians and fraudsters will make sure of that.

Saving is also not worthwhile because: the next bubble, stock market crisis or currency reform is sure to come and take your savings. Or even better: the state will raise taxes again.

You only get out of every euro anyway41 cents , if you factor in direct and indirect taxes. You pay tax on money that has already been taxed and then pay tax on it again. Only completely stupid politician arseholes could come up with that.

If you then have to pay interest on the loan, you have nothing left. And that's exactly how it's meant to be, so that you stay nicely trapped in this shit system.

And for what? So that you can go to the doctor for free, and because everything is so nice and clean in Shithole-Germany, or because everything is so nice and "safe"? almost

What a joke! Look around you. The money you're paying is being wasted on some run-of-the-mill, knife-wielding skilled labour and overpriced dodgy stuff, but not on what's important - namely our pensions, schools, security, police and a functioning infrastructure.

So even in old age, you won't have the opportunity to break out and lead the life you want. Because: there is nothing left, or what there is, **is no longer worth** anything!

Do you notice anything? Yes, exactly, I've just described your life. Didn't you?

When you realise this, you only have three options:

Option 1: You don't change anything, stay in the rut, make the best of it and enjoy the few nice moments until the lid is closed at some point. You resign yourself to the fact that you once acan go on holiday for three weeks year, but soon you won't be able to afford it anyway without taking out a loan! You simply continue to live from weekend to weekend.

Option 2: You stop working, quit your job, cancel your loans, go bankrupt, live only on benefits, are debt-free after three years and live like an ascetic on a low level, but are free of all obligations.

Option 3: You turn your back on this country and its moronic policies and emigrate to a country where you can still live. Find a job that pays enough to live well, even part-time. Preferably to a country where there are decidedly fewer people. I think that this squatting on top of each other in Germany makes people aggressive. If you didn't see a neighbour for weeks on end, you'd probably be happy if someone came over and visited you. A completely different mindset.

I often think back to a visit to the small island of Pserimos in the Aegean. At the top of a cliff stood a simple house, built from light-coloured stones that had absorbed the Mediterranean sun. From the terrace you could look directly out over the vast bay, the deep blue of the Aegean stretched to the horizon and the air was filled with a calm that is hard to find in my hectic world. I remember the gentle wind blowing through the olive trees and the feeling of complete isolation from everything else in my life.

My dream has always been to live in a house like this one day. A place where time seems to pass more slowly, where everyday life with its demands, constant expectations and the hunt for success has no place. There, I imagined, I could calm down, organise my thoughts and focus on the essentials. A life without the constant pressure to achieve something or prove who I am. Just the sea, the wind, the sun and the simple things in life.

View of the Aegean Sea from the terrace of the house.

But this dream will probably always remain a dream. Not because it would be impossible to own this house or because Pserimos would be too far away. But for exactly the reasons I have already mentioned:

The expectations I have of myself, the life I have built, the responsibilities I have - all of this keeps me trapped in a reality that rarely lets me go. Even if I had the money and the time to realise this life, what good would it do me if the inner doubts and the constant urge for confirmation still gnaw at me?

I often think that it's not just the place that attracts me, but the idea of simply escaping, of leaving it all behind. But even if I were sitting on this terrace, looking out over the Aegean, I probably wouldn't find the peace that I long for so much. Because the real conflict is not in the outside world, but in myself. It is the constant struggle between what I want to be and what I have become. Between the dreams I had and the reality I had to accept.

And so this dream remains a dream, because I know deep down that the true path to the peace I seek is not through geographical escape, but through an inner confrontation with myself.

Nevertheless, I hold on to this idea. Perhaps not as a goal that I will achieve one day, but as a symbol of the desire to actually be able to let go one day. Not just the daily grind, but also the inner struggles. Maybe I'll never live in a house on a cliff in the Aegean, but maybe one day I can find the peace I've always dreamed of there - no matter where I am.

And that's why I'm telling you: "Fuck the bucket list, fuck you, bucket list!"

For my part, I have realised what is going on and nobody needs to tell me about missed opportunities or failures. Not even about shattered dreams. I decide for myself what has burst, not others.

If the book is too crass or offensive in places, I apologise. It was never my intention to hurt anyone or cause offence. My aim was to describe my experiences at the time as authentically as possible - raw, honest and unfiltered, as I felt them at the time. This also includes a somewhat coarse slang that some would describe as "Berlin redneck big mouth". This way of expressing myself is part of my background, it is direct, blunt and sometimes harsh.

I decided to keep this tone because I think it best conveys what I've been through. The feelings, the anger, the hurt - you can't always put all that into soft words. It wouldn't be real. In a life that is often full of complexity and contrasts, this direct language was reflected and it helped me to organise and process my emotions.

So if some passages seem too blunt or provocative, I ask for your understanding. Sometimes life is not just black and white, but loud, unruly and unembellished. It is important to me to tell the truth of my own story as I experienced it - not to shock, but to be honest. And sometimes that requires a bit more rough edges.

With scratches through a difficult time

If you have read this book up to this point, I would first like to thank you. I know it has come across as very pessimistic and sarcastic in places. I'm sure you've often said to yourselves: "What kind of idiot is this?"

I think you're right to think that. Because my life has been anything but normal or average at times. But that's what life is all about. Not many people are granted the opportunity to follow such a path. I've experienced a lot, made a lot of mistakes, but in the end I'm sure I've also made some good decisions.

The first step towards a better future was to recognise who you are and why things are going the way they are. Only then is it possible to change.

Reflection and realisation

"Life is lived forwards and understood backwards." - Søren Kierkegaard

This quote from the Danish philosopher Søren Kierkegaard aptly describes how it is often only in hindsight that we realise the significance of events and decisions in life. Looking back on my own experiences, I now realise more clearly why I took certain paths and made certain mistakes. This reflection was essential for my further development and growth.

The importance of errors

"The greatest glory in life is not in never falling, but in getting up every time." - Nelson Mandela

Mistakes and setbacks are inevitable parts of life. However, they also offer us the greatest learning opportunities. Nelson Mandela emphasised the importance of getting up again after a fall. There have been many moments of failure in my life, but getting back up and moving on each time has ultimately made me stronger.

Self-realisation and knowledge

"The only thing we have to fear is fear itself." - Franklin D. Roosevelt

Fear can often prevent us from realising our full potential and making courageous decisions. Franklin D. Roosevelt reminded us that fear is often our greatest enemy. Overcoming my own fears was a crucial step on my path to self-realisation. It was only when I learnt to confront my fears and face them that I could truly live freely and authentically.

The search for meaning

"He who has a why to live can bear almost any how." - Friedrich Nietzsche

Friedrich Nietzsche's famous quote emphasises the importance of a deep, inner meaning or purpose in life. My own journey has often been characterised by a search for meaning. Understanding why I live and what my purpose is has helped me to overcome even the most difficult challenges. It is this sense of purpose that drives us and gives us the strength to persevere.

Resilience and endurance

"It's not the mountain we conquer, but ourselves." - Sir Edmund Hillary

Resilience and perseverance are key components in overcoming difficult times. The mountaineer Sir Edmund Hillary, who was the first to climb Mount Everest, knew that the greatest challenge is often to overcome one's own limitations. In my life, I have learnt time and time again that it is not the external circumstances that define us, but our ability to keep going despite adversity.

Acceptance and change

"The only constant in life is change." - Heraclitus

Change is inevitable and constant. The Greek philosopher Heraclitus recognised this thousands of years ago. My life has been characterised by many changes and I have often tried to fight against them. But the more I learnt to accept and even welcome change, the more I was able to develop and grow.

The power of self-love

"You yourself, like everyone else in the entire universe, deserve your love and affection." - Buddha

Self-love is the key to a fulfilled life. We are often our own harshest critic. Buddha teaches us that self-love and self-acceptance are essential. In my life, I have learnt to love myself, with all my flaws and imperfections. This self-acceptance has helped me to make peace with my past and look positively into the future.

Community and support

"No man is an island." - John Donne

The English poet John Donne reminds us that we are all connected and need support. During the most difficult times of my life, I have learnt the importance of having a strong community and supportive relationships. Friends, family and mentors have been my rocks in the storm, helping me to persevere and keep going.

The journey continues

"It's never too late to become what you could have been." - George Eliot

This thought by George Eliot is an encouraging mantra for anyone who feels they have come too late. It's never too late to change, set new goals and live the life you've always wanted. My own journey is proof that change and growth are possible at any time, regardless of the past.

Ultimately, I now have a wonderful life. I may not have been able to fulfil my dreams, but I have a family that loves me, a job that I enjoy, colleagues who like me, friends who enjoy spending time with me and, most importantly, a wife for whom I am the centre of attention. I can enjoy myself again and am happy with my life.

The menopause is and has been an ordeal, mentally and physically. I hope I've been able to help you a little.

My mate Tino - a few words from him

My life during the menopause

I never thought I would ever talk about something like menopause. To be honest, I didn't even know that men could have a menopause. But now, at the age of 55, I'm in the middle of it and want to share my story.

It all started a few years ago when I realised that I was constantly tired. I used to be full of energy and could easily cope with long working days and strenuous workouts. But suddenly I felt exhausted, even after a full night's sleep. At first I blamed it on stress at work and my increasing age, but when the tiredness didn't subside, I started to worry.

There were also constant mood swings. I was irritable and could get upset over the smallest things. This was not at all typical of me, and of course my wife and children noticed it too. We argued more often and I often felt misunderstood and isolated. This emotional instability was scary and I wondered what was wrong with me.

My sex life also suffered. My interest in sex decreased significantly and when the time came, I had difficulties getting an erection. It was frustrating and embarrassing. I felt less masculine and began to feel ashamed of my problems.

After living with these symptoms for some time, I decided to see a doctor. My urologist, Dr Heitkamp, patiently listened to my complaints and suggested checking my testosterone levels. The result confirmed what I had already feared: my testosterone level had dropped significantly.

Dr Heitkamp explained to me that I was going through the male menopause, also known as the andropause. He explained that this was a natural process in which testosterone production decreases, similar to women going through the menopause. This realisation was a shock for me, but at the same time a relief because I now knew that my symptoms had a cause.

We discussed various treatment options and I opted for testosterone replacement therapy. This therapy helped to improve my energy and general well-being. My mood also stabilised and I felt more like myself again. My sex life also normalised, which also benefited my relationship with my wife.

In addition to the medical treatment, I began to adapt my lifestyle. I paid more attention to my diet, reduced stress and emphasised regular exercise. These changes made a big difference. I felt fitter and healthier and was better able to cope with the challenges of everyday life.

Another important aspect was social support. I began to talk openly with my family and close friends about my situation. It was liberating to realise that I wasn't alone and that other men felt the same way. These conversations helped me to feel less isolated and boosted my self-confidence.

Looking back, I am grateful that I had the courage to seek help and talk openly about my problems. The male menopause is a topic that is still talked about far too little, but it is real and affects many of us. It's important that we men support each other and talk openly about our experiences.

Today, I feel more balanced again and can enjoy life, despite the challenges that the menopause has brought with it. If my story helps even one man to find the courage to seek support and talk openly about his experiences, then sharing my experiences will have been worthwhile.

Me and cheating - nope, cancelled

One night, when I was once again feeling plagued by tiredness and mood swings, I decided to go out on my own. I knew that my friends Alex and Tom often went to striptease bars, and although I had never considered it for myself before, the idea of trying something new appealed to me.

I never cheated, unlike Alex, who regularly cheated on his wife. But the desire for other women was always there, even though I never wanted to cheat on my wife. That's why I decided to go to a striptease bar - it seemed like a safe way to fulfil my fantasies without actually being unfaithful.

That evening, I went to one of the trendiest striptease bars in the city. The dim lighting and loud music helped me to forget my worries for a moment. I sat down at the bar, ordered a whisky and let my gaze wander round the room. An attractive woman was dancing on stage, her movements captivating the attention of everyone in the room.

While I was sitting there enjoying my drink, one of the dancers came up to me. She was breathtakingly beautiful, with long, dark hair and a seductive smile. "Would you like a private dance ?" she asked in a voice that sent a shiver down my spine.

Hesitantly, I nodded and followed her into a separate area. The room was smaller and more intimate, with soft sofas and dimmed lights. She began to dance and for a moment I forgot all my problems and the stress that had been haunting me for months. Her movements were mesmerising and I couldn't help but lose myself in the moment.

But during the dance, thoughts flashed through my mind. I thought about my wife at home, the years we had spent together and the difficulties we had overcome together. Although I enjoyed the dance, I felt guilty at the same time. I knew that this was not the way to resolve my inner conflicts.

After the dance, I thanked the dancer and left the bar. As I stepped out into the cool night, I felt a mixture of relief and regret. I was glad that I hadn't really been unfaithful to my wife, but I also realised that these experiences were only a temporary outlet for my problems.

I decided that I needed to do more to understand and address the causes of my inner turmoil. It was clear that I needed to talk to someone about my feelings and my fears - perhaps a therapist or a close friend. This experience in the striptease bar was a wake-up call that I needed to face my problems instead of suppressing them.

From that day on, I started to deal with my feelings more intensively and look for long-term solutions. I talked more with my wife and sought professional help. These decisions helped me to regain my balance and strengthen my marriage.

The memory of that evening remains etched in my mind, not as a moment of pleasure, but as a turning point in my life. It was the moment when I realised, , that I had to take responsibility and proactively work on my well-being instead of running away from my problems.

Alex the Hallodry -Romance before Bromance

One evening I decided to take my wife out for a nice dinner. We had been dealing with a lot of challenges lately and I thought a romantic evening would do us good. We chose a chic restaurant in the city centre that was known for its cosy atmosphere and excellent cuisine.

We had just ordered our main course when I recognised a familiar figure in the corner of my eye. It was Alex, my best friend, who had just entered the restaurant. But he wasn't there with his wife - at his side was a strikingly attractive woman who was definitely not his wife. They were laughing and holding hands, obviously in an intimate mood.

My heart skipped a beat. I knew that Alex had affairs, but I had always managed to stay out of his escapades so far. His wife was a dear friend of my wife and the tension between loyalty to my friend and honesty towards my wife was constantly present.

"Isn't that Alex?" my wife suddenly asked, half-turning round to get a better look. I quickly grabbed her hand and gently pulled her back. "Let's not pry," I said, hoping to divert her attention. But her suspicious look showed that she had already become suspicious.

"Why are you behaving so strangely?" she asked, looking at me piercingly. I could feel my face getting hot. "I just want us to enjoy our evening," repliedI and tried to remain calm. But a storm was raging inside.

During the rest of the evening, I tried to distract my wife and keep her from away . We changed seating positions several times and I made sure she didn't see him again. Every time she asked why I was so nervous, I made up a new excuse. I felt miserable lying to her, but I didn't want her to get caught up in AlexAlex's mess.

After dessert, I suggested that we treat ourselves to dessert at home and have a cosy film night. My wife agreed, but I could see she wasn't convinced. We left the restaurant and I was relieved when we were finally in the car and on our way home.

At home, my wife asked again: "Tell me the truth, did you know that Alex was having an affair?" I hesitated, but eventually nodded. "Yes, I knew it. But I didn't want you to know because I thought it would incriminate you."

"Of course it burdens me," she said, "not only because he's cheating on our girlfriend, but also because you knew and didn't tell me."

These words struck me deeply. I had thought I was protecting my wife, but in reality I had violated her trust. I apologised and promised to be more honest in future.

That evening was a turning point for me. I realised that being loyal to a friend didn't mean supporting or covering up their bad decisions. From then on, I decided to put my values and integrity first, even if it meant having difficult conversations and speaking honest truths.

Alex and I have since spoken about his affairs and I made it clear to him that I could not support his behaviour. He had to make his own decisions, but I knew that I would no longer "hold out" if it came at the expense of honesty and trust in my own relationships.

Loneliness in old age - How men can prevent social withdrawal

Loneliness in old age is an issue that affects many men, but few talk about it openly. While women often maintain close social networks to help them cope with ageing, many men are not used to sharing their feelings and needs in social circles. The result is often a gradual social withdrawal, which is exacerbated in old age - be it through retirement, children growing up or the loss of a partner or close friends. But loneliness is not inevitable. With the right attitude and a little courage to change, social withdrawal in old age can be prevented.

Why men get lonely in old age

There are many reasons why men tend to withdraw socially as they get older. One of the main reasons is the role that many men take on throughout their lives. Men often define themselves strongly by their occupation, their status and their ability to provide for their family. When these roles disappear in old age - whether through retirement or the end of parental duties - many men feel useless or lose their purpose in life. They have often focussed so much on their work and family that friendships or social networks have been neglected over the years.

In addition, many men are used to solving problems on their own. The desire for independence and self-determination is deeply rooted in the traditional male image. Feelings are not readily shared with others, and for many, accepting help is seen menas a sign of weakness. However, this attitude leads to men cutting back on their social connections rather than seeking new friendships or deeper social contacts. The result is a gradual withdrawal that can end in isolation.

The loss of close people, whether through the death of a partner or the drifting apart of friendships over time, also increases the feeling of loneliness. Many men find it difficult to make new friends or engage in new social activities as they get older, as this requires a certain degree of vulnerability and openness - qualities that they have often suppressed in the course of their lives.

The consequences of loneliness

Loneliness in old age is not only an emotional challenge, but also has tangible health consequences. Studies show that chronic loneliness increases the risk of cardiovascular disease, depression and dementia. It's a vicious circle: loneliness leads to emotional stress, which in turn affects physical and mental health. Life expectancy can also be shortened by social isolation. But although the consequences of loneliness are well known, many men find it difficult to break this cycle.

Loneliness not only has an impact on health, but also on self-image. Men who feel socially isolated in old age often doubt their value and importance in society. They feel superfluous or no longer needed. This inner withdrawal reinforces the feeling that they can no longer contribute and prevents men from actively seeking new social connections.

Ways out of loneliness: preventing social withdrawal

However, loneliness does not have to be the inevitable fate of old age. There are many ways in which men can actively combat social withdrawal and organise their lives in old age in a fulfilling and social way. The first and perhaps most important step is to realise that loneliness is not a sign of personal failure. It is a condition that affects many - but it can be changed.

Openness to new friendships Many men believe that friendships are only formed in youth and that it is difficult to make new contacts in old age. But the opposite is true: there are numerous opportunities to make new friends in later life. Whether through sports groups, clubs or hobbies - social networks can also be maintained and built up in old age. An open and positive approach to new encounters is the key to breaking down old barriers.

Active participation in groups and clubs Men who are actively involved in clubs or groups stay socially connected for longer. Whether it's a sports club, a book club or a walking group - shared interests unite and promote a sense of community. The advantage of such groups is that they enable regular meetings and thus maintain social contact. Getting involved in voluntary work or charitable projects can also be a great way to stay active and meet new people.

Discover new hobbies Old age offers the chance to do things that you may not have had time for during your working life. Discovering new hobbies, be it painting, making music or crafts, not only opens up creative freedom, but also new social networks. Sharing interests and learning together often creates a strong bond with other people who share similar passions.

The importance of neighbourhood and community Many men underestimate the importance of their immediate surroundings. The neighbourhood can be an important social resource. Regular conversations with neighbours or participation in community activities in the area promote social contacts. In many towns and communities, there are initiatives and programmes aimed at bringing older people closer together. It is worth taking advantage of these opportunities and being an active part of the community.

Using technology to stay connected Although using technology can be a challenge for many men as they age, it can be a great way to stay in touch with family and friends. Video calling, social networking and online groups offer ways to maintain social relationships even over long distances. Those who take the time to learn these technologies can expand and maintain their social networks.

Talk openly about feelings Perhaps the most difficult but most important step in preventing loneliness is the willingness to talk about feelings. Many men see it as a weakness to admit loneliness or sadness. However, it is important to open up emotionally, especially in old age. Talking to a friend, family member or even a professional counsellor can help to break through inner isolation. There is no shame in accepting help or talking about your needs.

Maintaining contact with the family The family is often the most important social resource, especially in old age. However, keeping in touch with children and grandchildren sometimes requires initiative and the will to actively participate in their lives. Joint activities, regular visits or simply a phone call can help to strengthen family ties. Even if the children are now grown up and busy, the family remains an important anchor against loneliness.

Drugs & Rock 'n' Roll - Never ever

I've never touched hard drugs in my life. For me, that includes coke, marijuana and other devilish stuff. It's always been a taboo for me because I hate losing control. You certainly need a certain predisposition to touch the stuff and think it's great. I never needed anything like that, not even cigarettes. The only thing is perhaps a good Cuban cigar at Christmas or on holiday.

What I always liked, however, was a good whisky or rum. But only up to a certain point. I've never been so drunk in my entire life that I couldn't find my way home.

Most of the time, it doesn't go beyond being tipsy. However, when the pressure was at its greatest, I hardly ever missed a day when I didn't have a whisky in the evening. Or half a litre of beer. My wife often asked me if I was slowly turning into an alcoholic. I didn't realise it myself, but in the end I was half-drunk almost every evening. I just needed it to wind down and calm my mind.

When I had a bit of a buzz, I could definitely fall asleep better. That's definitely the dangerous thing about alcohol. Ultimately, the body always needs larger quantities for the effect to occur.

So the step to alcoholism is certainly not far away. It was often the case that when my wife asked me if we wanted to have a glass of wine, she drank one glass and I drank the rest of the bottle. Of course, at some point she no longer wanted to have a nice glass of wine with me because it always ended in a drunken orgy.

I only realised this after about a year and then banned alcohol to calm down. Instead, I started putting on headphones and listening to audio books. It's like when your parents read you a fairy tale before going to bed. I usually fell asleep while listening to it and was completely relaxed in no time.

The consequences of alcohol consumption

Alcohol has a profound effect on the human body and mind. What begins as an occasional indulgence can quickly develop into a destructive habit that affects both physical health and mental well-being.

Physical effects:

Liver: The liver is the main organ that breaks down alcohol. With regular consumption, the liver has to work harder to metabolise the alcohol, which can lead to liver inflammation and, in the long term, to cirrhosis or liver cancer. The liver cells are damaged and scarring of the liver tissue can occur, which significantly impairs the function of the organ.

Heart: Alcohol consumption can damage the heart. In the long term, it can lead to high blood pressure, cardiac arrhythmia and an enlarged ventricle. Chronic alcohol abuse increases the risk of heart attacks and strokes.

Gastrointestinal tract: Alcohol irritates the stomach lining and can lead to gastritis and stomach ulcers. It also impairs the absorption of nutrients in the intestines, which can lead to deficiency symptoms and weight loss.

Pancreas: Alcohol can inflame the pancreas, which can lead to pancreatitis. This inflammation can be acute or chronic and can have serious consequences for digestion and blood sugar levels.

Immune system: Regular alcohol consumption weakens the immune system, which increases susceptibility to infections. The body is less able to fight bacteria and viruses, which can lead to more frequent and more severe illnesses.

Psychological effects:

Brain: Alcohol acts as a depressant on the central nervous system. In the short term, it leads to reduced inhibition and a feeling of relaxation. In the long term, however, it can damage the brain, leading to memory loss, concentration problems and permanent cognitive impairment.

Mood and behaviour: Alcohol alters neurotransmitters in the brain, which can lead to mood swings, anxiety and depression. These changes can also promote aggressive behaviour and an increased tendency towards risky actions.

Addictive behaviour: Alcohol can quickly become addictive. The body develops a tolerance, which means that you have to drink more and more to achieve the same effect. This can lead to a vicious circle of dependence and withdrawal symptoms when alcohol consumption is reduced or stopped.

Long-term consequences:

The long-term consequences of alcohol abuse are serious and often irreversible. Chronic illness, mental decline and social isolation are just some of the possible effects. The physical damage can lead to early death, while the psychological and social consequences significantly reduce the quality of life.

Alcohol offers a deceptive refuge that ultimately does more harm than good. Losing control means not only harming yourself, but also negatively impacting the lives of those around you. It's a long, hard road to overcoming addiction and restoring health, but it's a necessary step to living a fulfilling and healthy life.

Healthy alternatives to alcohol

Reaching for the bottle may seem like an easy solution to cope with the stress of everyday life and relax. But as we have seen, alcohol does more harm than good in the long term. However, there are many healthy alternatives that can help reduce stress and promote relaxation without the negative consequences of alcohol abuse.

1. sport and exercise:

Regular physical activity is one of the most effective ways to reduce stress and improve general well-being. Exercise releases endorphins, the so-called happiness hormones, which promote feelings of relaxation and satisfaction. Whether running, swimming, cycling or yoga - there are countless ways to get your body moving and calm your mind at the same time.

2. meditation and mindfulness:

Meditation and mindfulness exercises are excellent techniques for calming the mind and living in the moment. By focussing on your breath and consciously noticing your own thoughts and feelings, you can learn to reduce stress and find inner peace. There are numerous apps and online courses that help you integrate meditation into your everyday life.

3. reading and audio books:

Immersing yourself in a good book or listening to an exciting audio book can be a wonderful way to escape from everyday life and relax. Books offer an escape into other worlds and can help take your mind off your worries. Audiobooks have the added benefit that you can listen to them anywhere, whether you're going for a walk, cooking or before going to sleep.

4. creative activities:

Creative activities such as painting, drawing, writing or making music can also contribute to relaxation. They offer the opportunity to express yourself and calm your mind at the same time. Creativity promotes a sense of fulfilment and helps to forget the stresses of everyday life.

5. social interactions:

Spending time with friends and family can be a valuable source of relaxation and well-being. Social support is important for reducing stress and feeling loved and valued. Shared activities, whether it's a game night, a meal together or simply a walk, can help to clear the mind and promote positive emotions.

6. relaxation techniques:

Techniques such as progressive muscle relaxation, breathing exercises or autogenic training can help to relax the body and calm the mind. These methods are easy to learn and can be used anywhere to reduce stress and relax.

7. nature and gardening:

Spending time in nature has a calming effect on body and mind. Whether it's a walk in the park, hiking in the mountains or simply sitting in your own garden - nature offers a wonderful opportunity to leave the stresses of everyday life behind. Gardening can also have a therapeutic effect and strengthen the feeling of connection with nature.

8. music and dance:

Music has a strong emotional effect and can help you to relax and lift your mood. Whether listening to soothing music, singing or dancing - music offers many ways to reduce stress and experience joy.

9. tea and herbs:

Instead of alcohol, a cup of calming herbal tea can be a soothing alternative. Herbs such as camomile, lavender or lemon balm are known for their relaxing properties and can help to calm the mind and promote sleep.

10. professional help:

Sometimes it is difficult to deal with stress and anxiety alone. In such cases, professional support from a therapist or counsellor can be helpful. Therapy and counselling offer tools and strategies to deal with stress and develop healthy coping mechanisms.

The journey to relaxation and stress relief without alcohol may be a challenge, but it's worth it. There are many healthy alternatives that not only calm the mind, but also promote physical well-being. By finding new ways to relax and unwind, we can lead more fulfilling and healthier lives.

Natural preparations to help you fall asleep

The struggle with sleep is a daily challenge for many people. Insomnia can have a significant impact on daily life, and turning to prescription sleep aids is often associated with side effects. Fortunately, there are a number of natural supplements that can help you fall asleep without causing the unwanted side effects that come with synthetic medications.

1. melatonin:

Melatonin is a hormone that is naturally produced by the body and regulates the sleep-wake cycle. Melatonin supplements can be particularly helpful when the natural sleep-wake cycle is disturbed, for example in the case of jet lag or shift work. Melatonin is taken in low doses and has few to no side effects when used in the short term.

2. magnesium:

Magnesium is an essential mineral that plays an important role in many bodily functions, including muscle relaxation and the regulation of the nervous system. Magnesium supplements can help to relax the body and improve sleep quality . They are available in various forms, including tablets, powders and transdermal applications (such as magnesium oil).

3. valerian:

Valerian is a herbal remedy that has been used for centuries to promote sleep and relieve anxiety. Valerian root is available in the form of capsules, tablets, tinctures and teas. It has a calming effect and can help you fall asleep faster and improve the quality of your sleep.

4. passion flower:

Passionflower is another herbal remedy known for its calming and anxiolytic properties. It is often used in combination with valerian and other calming herbs to promote sleep. Passionflower is available in the form of capsules, tablets, tinctures and teas.

5. l-theanine:

L-theanine is an amino acid that is mainly found in green tea. It has calming properties and can help promote relaxation without causing drowsiness. L-theanine supplements can help calm the mind and improve sleep quality, especially when taken before bedtime.

6 Ashwagandha:

Ashwagandha is an adaptogenic herb used in traditional Indian medicine (Ayurveda). It helps the body adapt to stress and promotes relaxation. Ashwagandha can help to lower cortisol levels and improve sleep quality. It is available in the form of capsules, powders and tinctures.

7. lemon balm:

Lemon balm is another calming herb that has been used for centuries to promote sleep and relieve stress. It has mild sedative properties and can be taken in the form of capsules, teas and tinctures.

8. lavender:

Lavender is known for its calming and sleep-inducing properties. Lavender oil can be used in a diffuser to calm the room or applied directly to the skin (diluted with a carrier oil). Lavender tea can also have a relaxing effect and promote sleep.

9. glycine:

Glycine is an amino acid that acts as a neurotransmitter in the central nervous system. It has a calming effect and can help to improve the quality of sleep. Glycine is available in powder and capsule form and can be taken before bedtime.

10. camomile:

Camomile is one of the best known herbs for promoting sleep. Chamomile tea is a simple and pleasant way to relax before bedtime. Chamomile has mild sedative properties and can help calm the mind and improve sleep quality.

These natural supplements offer a gentle and effective way to promote sleep and improve sleep quality without the side effects often associated with prescription sleep aids. However, it is always advisable to consult a doctor before taking any new supplements, especially if you already have health problems or are taking other medications. With the right approaches and aids, the path to restful sleep can be made much easier.

Love-Letter - the biggest fool of us

The letter my wife wrote to me after my affairs came to light.

"I've always waited for you to finally be ready. Waited for your insecurity to disappear, waited for you to talk to me, to really see me and decide in my favour. Waited for you to recognise my true value. And if I had allowed you to carry on as before, I would probably still be waiting today.

I wanted to give us so many chances. Maybe I've already done that. Maybe even too many. I hoped and waited so much that you would change, that you would finally notice me and realise how great we could be together if only you had given us a real, honest chance. But you could never do that, could you? You were so emotionally hurt and damaged that you always kept me away from your heart.

You were everything I dreamed of. You saw how deep my love for you was, and yet you often used this fact to your advantage. I was never at the top of your priority list and you often made me feel that. I was someone who was content with the scraps of your attention and affection. That was my biggest mistake, because I allowed you to treat me badly. By settling for that, I became nothing more than an option. And that is the lowest thing you can mean to someone you care about.

By settling for less than I deserved, I hurt myself again and again. Every time I stayed by your side, I broke my heart again. I shed so many tears until I realised that I no longer felt myself. I gave you everything - love, understanding, respect and devotion. And you never tried to do the same. You just wore me down. You took me for granted, as if there were no consequences. You just assumed that you could go on like this forever.

At some point, you may have realised yourself that I would have had enough at some point. But I had hoped that you would recognise that moment before it was too late. Every time I did something for you, I thought it would bring us closer. But in truth, it only took me further away from you. I tried to be there for you when you needed me, even though you never let me fully into your life.

I didn't want to change you, I just wanted you to love me as much as I love you. I always listened to you, tried to understand and fulfil your needs. I did everything I could to save our love because I really believed that we could make it work. But in the end, I felt empty. I was strong for so long, but at some point I couldn't do it anymore.

I fought for us because I thought you were worth it. But at the same time, I realised that I had lost myself in the process. But when we were on the brink of separation, something happened. You changed. You started to really see me, started to do the things I had wanted for so long. You started to love me - the way I had always dreamed of."

Love letter for the 13th wedding anniversary - One year after the affair was discovered

"My beloved darling,

Maybe I'm not the dream woman you've always imagined, but I can tell you one thing: I'm the woman who wraps you in clean clothes.

I'm the one who warms you when you're cold. I am the one who caresses you when you are looking for rest and relaxation. I am the one who holds you when you are sad. I am the one who cares for you when you are ill. I am the one who has your back no matter what.

I am the one who never gave up on you. The one who always stayed by your side, even in those moments when it looked like we were going to lose each other. I am the one who loves you from the bottom of my heart. I am the one who catches you when you fall, who helps you when you get stuck.

What does 'dream woman' mean? For me, it means that I am the woman who will stay by your side, come what may. I love you, not because you're perfect, but because you've shown me that you're ready to change. All the best for your 13th wedding anniversary."

On holiday in Turkey, I booked a cabana for us for an evening on the beach. The hotel staff had decorated the cabana beautifully with a heart of roses, flares and fairy lights. I had organised a five-course menu for us, with all the trimmings. It was perfectly planned and I wanted to surprise her with it.

Instead of going to the hotel restaurant for dinner as usual, I took her by the hand and led her towards the beach. She looked at me with a questioning look and asked on the way: "Honey, what's going on? Where are you taking me?" I just grinned and said: "Just let yourself be surprised."

When we arrived at the cabana, she stopped. Her eyes widened and she put her hand over her mouth. She was overwhelmed by the sight of all the lights, the flowers and the lovingly laid table. She turned to me and her eyes were full of tears.

"Honey," she said in a trembling voice, "no one has ever done anything like this for me before." Then she burst into tears, but they were tears of joy. She was visibly touched and moved. "You're so sweet, I love you," she whispered and fell into my arms.

We spent an unforgettable evening, just the two of us, with the sound of the waves in the background and the warm sand beneath our feet. It was one of those moments when you realise that having this person by your side is exactly the right thing to do.

This love letter was the second in my life that really touched me deeply. At that moment, I finally realised what a strong woman I have by my side. How lucky I am and how grateful I should be for the second and last chance she gave me. When I think about what our lives would be like today if we had split up, I realise that it would probably have ended in disaster for both of us. I couldn't have imagined going through life alone.

I realise today that I should have acted much earlier. If I had had the knowledge back then that I have today, I would have been much quicker to get help.

You can't do everything with yourself. But we men often tend to do just that. We think we can solve our problems on our own, without outside help. But sometimes that just isn't possible. Some things you can't teach yourself. It's like learning a new trade: you get help from the DIY store to get the right materials and tools - and to avoid making mistakes.

Only when it comes to our own inner problems are we often too proud or too cowardly to ask someone for advice. Perhaps this is because we have been programmed for thousands of years to fight alone and look after our families. This problem-solving strategy is deeply ingrained in us. But times have changed and we have to realise that we can no longer do everything on our own.

In recent years, I have often realised that my assessments were wrong. Life has become too complex to provide simple answers. And if you make things too easy for yourself, you end up with rubbish. My wife has become my best counsellor - and she always has been. I just never really listened to her. She has a clear view of things and, surprisingly, always gives me the right advice. Especially when it comes to my poor judgement of character.

If I had listened to her earlier, I would have been spared a lot. The old saying "Behind every successful man is a strong woman" has proven to be true. I always thought it was just a cliché, but after all these years I have to admit that it's true. Women often have a different perspective on things - and that's often exactly what we men need.

Over the last few months, I've been thinking a lot about myself and my marriage. I'm curious to know how other men and their wives have experienced the menopause. Maybe we've all gone through similar challenges, maybe completely different ones. I would be interested to hear about your experiences. Feel free to write to me and share your stories. After all, we are all on this journey and perhaps we can learn from each other.

I'm sure that this strong woman will stay by my side forever. What kind of great person forgives such rubbish? I'm really lucky to such ahave loyal, honest and lovable partner by my side. She is my rock and I know that I wouldn't be the man I am today without her.

On a city trip to Istanbul in 2023, I wanted to show her how much I love and appreciate her. In the Hagia Sophia, surrounded by thousands of people, I got down on one knee in front of her and proposed to her. I asked her to marry me a second time - a sign that

I wanted to renew our promise. She had no idea of my plan, as I had carefully hidden the rings for weeks and planned the perfect moment.

When I pulled out the ring and recited my carefully memorised words, she was completely overwhelmed. I told her how much I loved her and what an incredibly loving person and what a great companion she is.

Tears streamed down her face and she only managed a shaky but firm "yes" before falling into my arms. She couldn't stop crying and I felt the same way. It was an extremely emotional moment that is etched in my heart forever.

The people around us clapped and cheered, some took photos, others filmed the scene. But none of that interested me. All that mattered to me at that moment was the woman in front of me, who I love more than anything. Her eyes, her smile, her warmth - she was the centre of my world.

If the people around us had known what a sinner I was and how much pain I had once caused this woman, they certainly wouldn't have cheered in this holy place. But for me it was a new beginning, a moment when I decided to be a better man - for her and for us.

New beginnings - the courage to change in the second half of life

I have already described my life path in detail in the previous chapters. Looking back, I realise that most men of my age certainly don't have the courage to change.

This is mainly due to the fact that entrenched routines and rigid thinking lead to change being seen as a threat rather than an opportunity. We get used to what we know and the unknown becomes a scary space that we avoid. But I have learnt that it is precisely this courage to change that is necessary in order to move forward not only in life, but also within ourselves.

In my case, it was the increasingly difficult business environment that finally led me to give up my self-employment after 30 years and return to as an employee atwork . It was not an easy decision. I had been my own boss for a long time, running my own business and making my own decisions. And suddenly I found myself in a situation where I had to fit back into a structure that was dictated by others. For many men, that would be unthinkable, especially after so many years of self-determination. But for me it was necessary. I had the feeling that I had reached a point in my independence where I was just going round in circles. The pressure was increasing and I realised that the joy I used to have in my work had long since disappeared.

Changes like these require courage. It means leaving old certainties behind and trying something new without knowing exactly what to expect. Many men my age are afraid of this because it seems easier to stick to the familiar. But for me, the change was a liberation. I felt like I had a clear head again, and although it wasn't easy to switch to being an employee after such a long time, I've never regretted it. I can only say that it was the right decision for me - one that I should have made much earlier. I'm sure that not many men make this step, especially after such a long time in a self-determined role. But those who have the courage to take on something new are often rewarded. Sometimes it's exactly what you need to find satisfaction and balance again.

Another thing that has led me to make profound changes in my life is the decision to keep my relationship exclusively monogamous. It's no secret that I've cheated and I know I'm not alone in this. Statistics show that one in three men in a committed relationship cheats - and there is probably an even higher number of unreported cases. What made me change? I think it was the realisation that my behaviour was not only destroying my marriage, but also myself.

I hope that my words here will fall on fertile ground and perhaps persuade one or two men to change their ways. Cheating may seem exciting at the time, but the price you pay for it is high. In my case, it led to me being mentally and emotionally absent from my partner. My mind was on other women, looking for the next "thrill", and in the meantime our marriage was becoming more and more damaged. It was as if I had built an invisible wall between us without really realising it. It was only when I was ready to question my behaviour and recognise the consequences that my cheating was having on our relationship that I was able to turn the corner.

Since I decided to stop cheating and focus all my attention and energy on my partner, our marriage has changed completely. Suddenly there was closeness, intimacy and trust again. The emptiness I had felt before disappeared and I realised that all the things I had been looking for in other women were actually in my own partnership all along. I just had to learn to see and appreciate them again.

It was certainly not an easy way to break out of old patterns, but it was the only right one. I'm glad that I managed to break away from my destructive behaviour in time before any more damage was done. Today, our relationship is harmonious and fulfilling - and that's not because I "gave up" anything, but because I finally realised what was really important.

Change is often associated with fear and uncertainty. We men tend to hold on to what we know, even if it harms us. But sometimes all it takes is that one moment of courage, that first step into the unknown, to steer your life back in the right direction. And if there's one thing I've learnt from my own experience, it's that it's never too late to make a fresh start.

Rituals are incredibly important in a functioning relationship. They provide stability, security and create a connection that can often get lost in everyday life. But is just as important **spontaneity - the salt in the soup**. Without it, life would become monotonous and predictable. **It's about creating shared memories** that you can hold onto in difficult times, memories that give you energy and joy in everyday life. That's what makes a relationship strong: this balance between consistency and small adventures that keep the spark alive.

One example: **We have introduced a fixed wellness day in our relationship.** Once a week, we treat ourselves to a nice, warm bath together, with candles, champagne and pure relaxation. It's so simple and yet so effective. In this moment, it's just about the two of us - no distractions, no everyday worries. It's a little ritual that brings us together again and again and gives us the opportunity to switch off completely. Sometimes it's precisely these little routines that make a relationship stable and strong. They provide a kind of anchor in the constant stream of everyday life.

But then there are the spontaneous things that liven up everyday life. The little surprises, the unexpected experiences that make your heart beat faster. I often think up spontaneous outings, usually on Sundays when we're both free and the week is behind us. Nothing big, nothing expensive - but always something that makes us laugh together, be amazed or simply enjoy our time together.

Sometimes it's a trip to the forest, a visit to a small café that we've never tried before or a trip to a lake where we simply enjoy the peace and quiet. **These excursions bring a breath of fresh air into our relationship** because they take us out of our routine and give us new experiences together.

It's not about reinventing the wheel every time or doing particularly spectacular things. **It's about the shared moments that come back to mind later and our put a smile on faces** . It is these moments that keep us going in difficult times. They remind us why we are together and how much fun we can have together, even in the simplest things.

The mixture of rituals and spontaneity is the key. The rituals give us stability, the spontaneity adds flavour. Both together ensure that we fall in love with each other again and again and that the relationship remains fresh and lively. Once you realise this, you realise how important it is to make time for each other - both for the little routines and for the spontaneous adventures.

Because at the end of the day, that's what it's all about: **creating shared memories that will carry us through the difficult phases and show us that life - and love - is made up of many small moments that are worth capturing.**

Mentor and role model - How men can inspire others during the menopause

The menopause is often a phase of reflection and inner upheaval. While many men struggle with questions about their own identity, ageing and physical changes during this time, there is also an opportunity to see this phase of life as a chance - an opportunity to make a difference not only for themselves, but also for others. This is because men can play a crucial role as mentors and role models during the menopause by sharing their life experiences and supporting the younger generation.

For many men, the idea of being a mentor does not come naturally. The classic image of a mentor who guides young men or colleagues often does not seem to be integrated into everyday life. But the role of the mentor is much more than that. It is about passing on wisdom, experience and perspectives gained over the course of a lifetime. Men in the menopause have precisely these life experiences and the ability to offer guidance to others. They can share what they have learnt over the years - in professional, family and personal areas - and thus help others to find their own way.

The importance of being a mentor

Mentors are not only advisors, but also role models. Through their own behaviour, they show how to master difficult situations, how to deal with setbacks and how to achieve success through consistency and adaptability. Men in the menopause have often experienced many such challenges - be it professionally, in relationships or in coming to terms with their own identity. These experiences make them valuable guides for younger men who may be just beginning to face these issues.

Being a mentor means being present - not only in the good times, but also when things get difficult. It's about admitting your own mistakes and weaknesses and showing others that they don't have to be perfect either. This openness is often what makes the biggest impression. Because while there is a lot of insecurity and striving for success in the younger generation, there is often a lack of realisation that setbacks are also part of life - and that you can learn and grow from these setbacks.

The power of listening

One of the most important skills of a mentor is listening. Especially in a world that is often hectic and noisy, having someone really listen and not just give advice is invaluable. Men in the menopause have often developed the patience and understanding needed to give the younger generations space for their own thoughts and concerns. It is not always easy to talk openly about fears and insecurities as a young man, especially in a society where masculinity is often equated with strength and invulnerability.

This is where men in the menopause can build a bridge by showing that true strength lies in being vulnerable. Sharing your own insecurities and doubts that you have experienced throughout your life can help young men to feel understood. It can encourage them to be more open about their own challenges and accept help when they need it.

Passing on wisdom

With ageing comes a certain wisdom that can only be acquired through lived experience. Whether it's career decisions, family responsibility or personal development - men in the menopause have often lived through these issues many times and can pass on their insights. Passing on this wisdom is a form of legacy that lasts beyond their own lifetime.

Being a mentor does not mean always having the right answers, but knowing that by asking the right questions you can also help others to find their own way. The willingness to listen and reflect, rather than just present solutions, is one of the most valuable qualities of a mentor. It's about getting others to think about their own goals, values and challenges - and helping them find their own direction.

A role model for composure and adaptability

Men in the menopause have often learnt an important lesson: life doesn't always go in a straight line. There are twists and turns, setbacks and surprises that take life in a direction you may not have expected. This ability to adapt and remain calm is something that younger men often still have to learn. They are often under pressure to achieve everything in a short space of time, and the idea that life takes time and patience is difficult for them.

Men in the menopause can serve as role models here by showing that life doesn't always go according to plan - and that this is okay. Composure and the ability to deal with change are key qualities they can impart. They can take the pressure off younger men by showing that it's okay if not everything is perfect straight away - that life is a process where it's just as important to accept setbacks and reorientate yourself.

The role in the family and the community

Men in menopause often also play an important role within the family and the community. In many cases, they are the "pillars" of their families, and their children or grandchildren look up to them. Again, they can inspire through their life experience and serve as role models for integrity, responsibility and compassion. It is about showing, not only through words, but above all through deeds, what it means to be there for others and to take responsibility.

Men can also play an important role in the community at this stage of their lives. Whether through volunteering, sharing expertise or simply offering to be there for others - there are many ways to act as a role model. Involvement in the community not only provides guidance for the younger generation, but also offers the men themselves a meaningful purpose in life. It gives meaning to their own existence and establishes a connection to the people around them.

Conclusion: being a mentor as fulfilment

The menopause is a time of upheaval and reflection, but it also offers the opportunity to help others find their way as a mentor and role model. Men in this phase of life often have a rich treasure trove of experiences that they can share with others. They can show younger men that it is not important to be perfect, but to be open, honest and willing to learn from their own mistakes.

Being a mentor is not about always having the right answers, but about helping others find their own answers. It means making a difference through listening, serenity and sharing wisdom - not only in the life of the mentor, but also in the lives of those they inspire. In this way, menopause can not only be a time of transition, but also a time to give back to the world and touch the lives of others in a profound way.

Financial provision - What men should consider during the menopause

There are few topics that men are as reluctant to talk about as money. It's almost a taboo. We often talk about successes, challenges and the ups and downs of life, but when it comes to financial provision, there is often silence. However, the topic of money means more than just security - it means freedom and independence. This aspect becomes particularly important in old age, when one's own strength diminishes and the opportunities to "make a difference" become increasingly limited. Retirement is suddenly within reach and the question of how well you have prepared for this transition comes to the fore.

For many men going through the menopause, this is a bitter realisation. Perhaps because life has not always gone according to plan. Personal setbacks, career crises or economic circumstances have prevented you from putting enough money aside. I am no stranger to this experience myself. Due to various setbacks in life, whether professional or personal, I have never managed to put enough money aside . And now that I'm approaching retirement age, I'm feeling the consequences. My pension will be at a low level, and that means I have to prepare myself for a radical cut.

The wake-up call during the menopause

The menopause is often a time for self-reflection, and this includes taking an honest look at your own financial situation. Many men who have worked independently for years suddenly find themselves in a situation where they don't have sufficient reserves. In my case - and I know that many other men feel the same way - external circumstances, crises or even the pandemic have caused the business to collapse. The dream of financial freedom has vanished into thin air, and instead we are faced with the question of **what to do next.**

It's a wake-up call. During the menopause, you suddenly realise that the time in which you can still make big leaps is getting shorter and shorter. You no longer have the energy and strength to start all over again. But that doesn't mean that all is lost. There are still ways to improve your financial situation or at least mitigate the worst-case scenarios.

What to do if the pension is not enough?

For many men, the question arises: **what happens if the pension is not enough?** In my case, this means that I will either have to emigrate or severely restrict myself in old age. Emigrating may sound like a radical step, but in countries with a lower cost of living, the money that isn't enough in Germany could go much further. Countries such as Spain, Portugal or even some Eastern European states offer more favourable living conditions and at the same time a pleasant climate for retirement.

For others, it may mean adjusting to a smaller home or a more frugal lifestyle. It's not an easy decision to make, especially if you've been used to a certain standard all your life. But this is where the most important point comes into play: **flexibility and adaptability.** The menopause is not just a period of physical and emotional change, but also a time when you have to learn to deal with the new realities of life - and that includes reorganising yourself financially.

How can you take precautions now?

For those who are lucky enough to still have a few years until retirement age, now is the right time to take action. There are various ways to make provisions for retirement even in the last years of your working life. These include, for example, investing in private pension insurance or pension products that are tax-incentivised in Germany. The Riester pension, Rürup pension or company pension schemes are instruments that can be used to supplement the statutory pension.

Another approach is to take a close look at your own spending. It may sound trite, but many men have developed habits over the course of their lives that are financially burdensome without realising it. Now is the time to take a critical look at your own consumer behaviour and make savings where possible. Sometimes even small changes, such as switching electricity providers or reviewing insurance policies, can create financial leeway that makes a difference in the long term.

The option of continuing to work part-time or freelance in old age can also be a sensible solution. Many men underestimate how valuable their professional experience is. There are numerous opportunities to continue using this expertise in an advisory capacity or on a freelance basis. This not only provides an additional source of income, but also keeps you mentally and physically fit.

The reality for former self-employed people

Former self-employed people are often hit particularly hard. Many of us have not built up sufficient pension provision because we have had to invest in our business time and again or have been affected by external crises. In recent years in particular, due to the pandemic and economic changes, many self-employed people have lost everything they had worked for over decades. The idea of suddenly finding yourself without sufficient financial resources after a lifetime of hard work is harrowing - but it is a reality for many.

For us self-employed people, it is particularly important to deal with the issue of pension provision at an early stage. In most cases, there is no automatic pension scheme like there is for employees, and this means that we are responsible for it ourselves. But even if you may have neglected this in your younger years, it's never too late to look at alternatives now. Starting late with pension products or reallocating assets can also help to stabilise your financial situation in old age.

Mental reset - a fresh start during the menopause

Menopause. For many men, this sounds like an "end". The end of youthful energy, top sporting performance or career advancement. But wait a minute, guys - who actually says that? The truth is: the menopause is not an end, but a turning point. It's a phase in which you can regroup, shed old baggage and start afresh with new goals. Sounds trite? Maybe so. But that's exactly the mental reset you need right now.

First of all, it's okay if you're feeling overwhelmed right now. Many of us experience old certainties crumbling during this time. The job that used to excite you suddenly feels like a dead end. You look in the mirror and wonder who that guy with the grey hair is. Your fitness is declining, your relationship is no longer going so well and the children - if you have any - have long since left home or are on the move. Then you find yourself in the middle of life and ask yourself: "What now?"

This is exactly where the opportunity lies. Because this phase forces you to pause and take stock. What was good? What really fulfilled you? And above all, what do you want to do with the time that lies ahead? Life is not a never-ending game, and this often becomes particularly clear to us men during the menopause.

It's not about throwing everything overboard or starting from scratch. It's about living more consciously. Maybe you've been successful in your job so far and have achieved everything you set out to do - but now you realise that something is missing. Or that what used to motivate you no longer gives you the same kick. That's normal. It doesn't mean that you've failed. It just means that you've grown - and that it's time to adjust your goals.

A mental reset means consciously taking time to think about your life. Not on the spur of the moment or over a beer with mates, but with real focus. Write down what you want for the next few years. Maybe you want to develop professionally, start a new hobby, rediscover an old passion or simply have more time for yourself and your health.

The good thing about the menopause is that it forces you to prioritise. Maybe you used to feel like you had to be the best at everything - at work, in sport, as a partner or father. But now is the time to be honest with yourself. It's perfectly okay not to be perfect everywhere. The trick is to find the things that are really important to you and prioritise them.

A mental reset can also mean letting go of old beliefs. The pressure to always be strong and invulnerable is one of them. Guys, let me tell you one thing: it's not weakness to aboutthink your insecurities or to get help when you need it. On the contrary, it shows strength.

Use this phase to reset your goals - without fear, without pressure. It's not about impressing the world, it's about living a life that fulfils you. Menopause is not a crisis, but an invitation to redefine your path. Go for it. Your reset button is waiting.

A few words at the end

Guys, I have no idea if you liked my book or, more importantly, if it really helped you. When I started writing this book, I struggled quite a bit. The whole process took over a year, and honestly, it wasn't easy to relive all the positive and negative events of my life. It sometimes felt like I was holding up a mirror to myself - and in many parts it was actually like a kind of self-therapy.

Writing has taught me a lot about myself, especially in relation to my often impulsive and destructive behaviour. I realised that many of these behaviours are not just to do with my menopause, but are deeply rooted in my past. The menopause didn't cause these behaviours, but it was a real **booster** - it increased my impulsiveness and aggression. Looking back, I can see more clearly where my problems lay and how the menopause brought everything to a head.

Although I've written a few books before - mainly non-fiction - this one was a real challenge. It's completely different to write about your own weaknesses and insecurities. Firstly, because I have no idea if it will resonate with readers and if it was worth all the effort. Secondly, because I'm really afraid of what friends, colleagues or

What people who know me will think when they find out what a complete horst I was at times. It's not easy to show yourself to be so vulnerable, especially when you've maintained the façade of the "strong man" for years.

But then I think to myself: **OK**, maybe I can draw on a quote from the Bible: "Why do you see the mote in your brother's eye, but do not notice the beam in your own eye?" (Matthew 7:3). Or, even better, another quote from Jesus: "Let him who is without sin among you cast the first stone" (John 8:7). Nobody is perfect, and I hope that other people will read my book with an open heart and understanding.

Over the last few months, my wife has constantly encouraged me to keep writing. She said it would be a great book, that there was nothing like it before and that it would certainly help many men my age.

Without her positive pressure, I might never have finished the project. She motivated me to keep going and the really helped me, even if there were moments when I just wanted to give up.

That's why I very much hope that **you**, my fellow men, as well as your partners, can relate to my experiences, my suffering, my misbehaviour and the conclusions I have drawn from them. I hope that my words will help you - be it to avoid making the same stupid mistakes as I did or perhaps to pause in time and reconsider your own behaviour. If I could prevent even one of you from falling into the same traps, that would be a huge success for me.

The truth is: **the menopause really hits us men hard**. Everything that once seemed safe - our body, our attitude to life, our psyche - is suddenly turned upside down and called into question. It's a time when a lot changes, and it's important to get through this phase of life with as few "bumps" as possible. But I promise you, it will pass. And when you do, you will be stronger and more grounded than ever before.

If the book came across as too crass or offensive in places, I would like to apologise. It was never my intention to offend anyone. I simply wanted to portray my experiences at the time as authentically as possible - with all the harsh tones that go with it. And yes, I admit that I sometimes wrote in "Berlin redneck big mouth" slang. But that's how I felt at the time, and that's how I wanted to convey it to you.

What I'm really interested in is: What experiences have you had with your menopause? How do you deal with the physical and emotional changes? Why don't you write to me, I look forward to any feedback. Maybe you have some tips that could help other men, or maybe you're looking for advice and support yourself. I firmly believe that we can help each other by talking openly and honestly about what moves us. We don't have to keep this topic hidden - on the contrary, the more we talk about it, the more we can learn from each other.

Thank you for reading the book. It was really important to me to share my experiences with you and I hope that it has helped you in some way - whether by opening up new perspectives or making you think. Let's talk openly about this phase of our lives, without shame and without fear. Because only then can we really emerge stronger and perhaps even start a new, more conscious chapter of our lives.

I look forward to hearing from you - whether you have questions, feedback or just want to share your own story. Write to me at alex@xoloxx.org. Let's start a dialogue that will take us all a step further.

Your Alex

Imprint
Alexander von Gruenau (sole trader)
Xoloxx online publishing house
Brandenburgische Strasse 149 P.O. Box 39
15366 Schöneiche bei Berlin | Phone +4917675675916 | E-Mail: alex@xoloxx.org
Web: https://www.maenner-in-der-midlife-crisis.de
Publisher: BoD · Books on Demand GmbH, In de Tarpen 42, 22848 Norderstedt, bod@bod.de
Print: Libri Plureos GmbH, Friedensallee 273, 22763 Hamburg
ISBN: 978-3-7693-2338-2